Silk Riders

Morgan, Gareth (Gareth H. T.)
Silk riders : Jo and Gareth Morgan's incredible journey on the trail of Marco Polo / by Gareth & Jo Morgan.
ISBN-13: 978-1-86941-775-8
ISBN-10: 1-86941-775-5
1. Morgan, Gareth (Gareth H. T.)—Travel—Silk Road. 2. Morgan, Jo—Travel—Silk Road. 3. Motorcycle touring—Silk Road. 4. Silk Road—Description and travel. I. Morgan, Jo. II. Title.
915.0443—dc 22

A RANDOM HOUSE BOOK
published by
Random House New Zealand
18 Poland Road, Glenfield, Auckland, New Zealand
www.randomhouse.co.nz

First published 2006. Reprinted 2006 (four times)

ISBN-13: 978 1 86941 775 8
ISBN-10: 1 86941 775 5

Text design: Sharon Grace
Cover design: Katy Yiakmis
Author photograph: Chris Coad
Map: Holly Roach
Printed in Australia by Griffin Press

Silk Riders

JO AND GARETH MORGAN'S INCREDIBLE JOURNEY ON THE TRAIL OF MARCO POLO

with John McCrystal

RANDOM HOUSE
NEW ZEALAND

Contents

BLACK SEA
Venice
ARAL SEA
CASPIAN SEA
CROATIA
BULGARIA
Korcula
Istanbul
TURKMENISTA
ITALY
Gallipoli
TURKEY
Ashgab
Tehran
GREECE
SYRIA
IRAN
MEDITERRANEAN SEA
IRAQ
SAUDI ARABIA

Route map

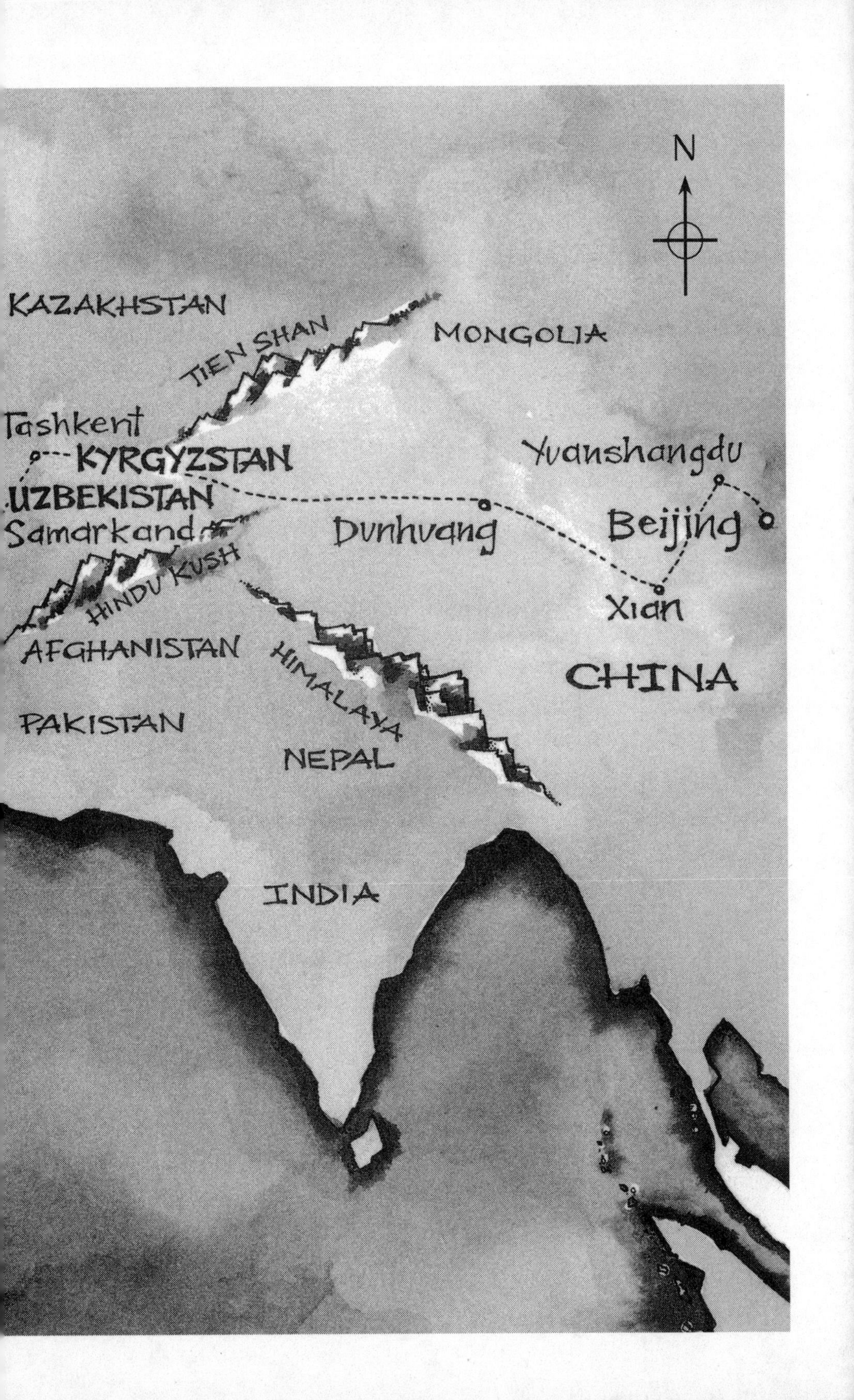
N
KAZAKHSTAN
TIEN SHAN
MONGOLIA
Tashkent
KYRGYZSTAN
Yuanshangdu
UZBEKISTAN
Samarkand
Dunhuang
Beijing
HINDU KUSH
Xian
AFGHANISTAN
HIMALAYA
CHINA
PAKISTAN
NEPAL
INDIA

Silk Road dreams

It all began one fine night in October 2001. A group of us — paying punters, and our guide Mike Ferris — were sitting around a fire, sipping red wine. It was a cool evening. The stars at this altitude had to be seen to be believed; we were at 4250 m, camped 275 km from Leh, one of the towns in the Indian Himalaya and capital of Ladakh or 'Little Tibet' as it is known. After listening to single-cylinder Enfields burbling all day, the quiet was sublime. Our muscles, more or less accustomed by now to the rigours of full days in the saddle, ached pleasantly. This wasn't too hard to take.

As always happens near the end of a motorcycle tour, our thoughts were turning to the next one. We asked Mike what was coming up in terms of future tours.

'Oh, I think we'll do the Silk Road,' he replied.

What, we wondered, was the Silk Road?

It turned out that Mike had done a bit of homework on the subject, and he filled us in. It was the ancient trade route — or, more accurately, the series of routes — between China and the West, along which various cultural and technological exchanges had taken place over the last 2000 years or more. Sericulture — the production of silk — had been underway in China since around 3000 BC, and while the fabric itself was traded west, reaching as far as Rome around the birth of Christ, the technology of silk production didn't spread outside China until around AD 400.

For the first few hundred years AD, the route along which silk and other commodities were traded enjoyed the protection of a number of the great empires and emperors of world history. It enjoyed one golden era during the Tang Dynasty from the 600s to the 900s, when China was unified and openly courting the world beyond its borders, and then another in the 1100s, when not only China but also much of the rest of the known world began to fall under the influence of the emperor of emperors, Genghis Khan. Under Genghis' successor, his grandson Kublai, the Mongol empire extended the Silk Road from the Chinese capital Xian in the east to Hungary in the west.

It was in 1292, during the reign of Kublai Khan, that the fabled Venetian traveller Marco Polo set out from Xanadu in China for the three-year journey back to his home town. He had spent 24 years travelling around the Great Khan's realm in the company of his merchant uncles and in the diplomatic service of the khan himself. Upon his return to Venice, he commemorated his adventures in a book that fired the dreams of travellers for the next 700 years, sometimes with unexpected results. It was Polo who brought back to Europe tales of the 'land of Beach', said to lie across the sea to the south of the Great Khan's domains, where gold was abundant and the inhabitants entirely ignorant of its value. These tales, in turn, prompted the Dutch East India Company to equip an expedition to the South Pacific under the command of Abel Tasman to locate this El Dorado, and it was in the execution of this endeavour that New Zealand was first discovered by Europeans.

Some modern scholars doubt that Marco Polo ever made the journey he describes in such lavish detail in his book, and the adventurer was met with similar scepticism in his own day, too. He earned the nickname 'Il Milione' — Teller of a Million Tales — in

Venice, and was considered by many to be the greatest bullshitter of his generation. Yet for all the scepticism in the West, Chinese researchers reckon there are important details in Polo's account — notably the names of three of Kublai Khan's court ambassadors — that align with the Chinese historical record, details Polo could not have learned unless it were, as he claimed, at first hand.

True or false, it's a magical story, drawing a single, shining thread through the greater part of human history, the rise and fall of empires, the ebb and flow of the great religions.

'That's the next trip I want to do,' Mike finished wistfully. 'The Silk Road from Turkey to China. It's a biggie. It would take a fair bit of organisation.'

We looked at one another, our eyes shining in the firelight. Wow, we were all thinking. Here we were all pumped up about having ridden from Delhi to Kashmir, and Mike's talking about Istanbul to Beijing. Now *that* would be an adventure.

'Count us in,' we said.

The fact is, like most true bikers, we're addicted to motorcycling and motorcycle touring. Jo practically grew up on bikes. And ever since he could grow one, Gareth has sported a biker moustache. Since we got married, we've taken every opportunity possible to get out into the countryside on our bikes. It's a great way to travel. You're independent. One of you is interested in, say, antiques. The other one isn't: he's interested in vintage-car museums. If you're together in a car, the one driving tends to accelerate when he sees an antique shop, or she points in the opposite direction and says 'Look at that!' when she sees a sign for a vintage-car museum. Well, on a bike you can do what you like. You can just peel off the route and have a look at whatever you fancy, play whatever music you like and just generally avoid all those things that tend to see families in cars arriving at their destination sour with one another. When we tour together, we probably spend more time stopping or detouring alone than we do together, and this is the beauty of it.

You occasionally hear people talk about motorcycling as freedom, and you're probably inclined to think they're wankers on the strength of it. But there's a sense in which it's true. You can cover the miles, but you're not insulated from your surroundings the way you are in a car. Not only can you see the world around you, you can feel the temperature change as you plunge into shaded cuttings, or cruise out onto a sunlit straight. You can certainly feel the weather. If it rains, you get wet. If it snows, your fingers freeze. It makes you feel much more vitally involved with the country you're passing through. You can smell it, too. Motorists miss out on this. You don't know you're alive until you've cruised through the sweet, heavy smell of silage on a New Zealand back-country road, or the hot smell of lupins or gorse or hay in summer in Central Otago.

And there's another component to it as well, harder to describe. Cars tend to be an extension of personal space for most people. On a bike, there's none of that. You're out there in the world, intimately involved with it without those territorial anxieties. It's a great feeling.

When the kids came along, we were determined it wasn't going to put an end to our biking. But we took 14 years and four infants away from two-wheelers before we plunged back in in 1990, buying two Harleys. There seemed little point in both of us sitting at home minding the kids with the bikes shining in the garage, just wishing we were touring. So we took turns. We each had our own group of mates. First Gareth fell in with a group who were interested in touring. Then Jo made contact with a completely separate group, who had two rules: no pillions, and no spouses. Hers is a big group, consisting of some engineers and practical dudes, and it took a little while for them to accept Jo. But after more than a few miles down the road, she'd proved herself and they became good mates. People would stare in amazement when this crowd of bikes would pull in — 35 blokes and one petite redhead — and take over an entire pub. People would shake their heads, unable to see the attraction for her. These, of course, are people who just don't understand the thrill of biking.

So when Gareth was off biking, Jo would be at home looking after the kids. When Gareth got back, it was Jo's turn, and this was the pattern. It wasn't ideal — it wasn't as much fun as touring together — but at least we were getting time in the saddle.

That Himalaya tour was the first big overseas biking trip we did. We followed it with another to the Andes just one year later in 2002. From the first day we, along with fellow Kiwi rider Dave Wallace who had also been in the Himalaya with us a year earlier, were badgering Mike about the Silk Road. How many people could go? How long would the trip take? Had he done any costings? When could we start? He looked as though he regretted ever opening his trap about the Silk Road.

There were 12 of us along on this South American trip, eight Australians and four Kiwis. Our route took us through Bolivia, Chile and Peru. Again, it was unforgettable. We marvelled at the high, barren plains of Bolivia, where people who are scratching the most precarious of livings in some of the worst farming country you can imagine wear the kinds of brightly coloured clothing you'd expect to see only on ceremonial occasions. Also in Bolivia, we crossed the Salar de Uyuni, a system of salt pans 20 times the size of Lake Taupo. Rainwater lay nearly 8 cm deep over the entire surface, so we ploughed up little bow-waves and raised rooster-tails of spray behind us: we could have pulled water-skiers! It was 80 km of the most surreal landscape we or any of the others had ever ridden through: heading into a sunset where sky and land were indistinguishable in a single broad band of red and gold . . . unforgettable. So too was coasting down the Amazon side of the Andes, a vivid contrast to the bleak countryside in the west.

There were, of course, the rough bits to go with the smooth: the poverty, particularly in Bolivia, which was distressing to behold; the bureaucracy at the borders, greatly exacerbated by corruption; the tedious hour we spent with screwdrivers chipping away the salt that had caked on the cooling fins on the front of our cylinder walls; the evening — among the coldest we've ever experienced — we spent on the roadside feeding tyre fragments, corn cobs, splinters from crates and anything else we could find to the fire we built while we waited for the support vehicle to catch us up after we ran out of fuel. And, of course, there were the 16 'involuntary dismounts' our group suffered on this trip. Two of them, including the most serious, were caused by one of the dangers motorcyclists face that are unique to this part of the world: forget dances with wolves, we're talking crashes with dogs. The mangy, evil-looking bastards are everywhere, liable to rush out and have a go at you anywhere, anytime. The worst 'off' left one of our poor Aussies — a bloke who had never suffered so much as a scratch in a motorcycle-racing career spanning 40 years — with broken ribs, a broken collarbone and, we found out later, a punctured lung. His injuries saw him spend three weeks in a Peruvian hospital and undergo two operations before being shipped home for a third. All part of the fun.

By the time we flew out of Peru, we were more determined than ever to do the Silk Road by bike. We subjected poor old Mike to an email barrage once we were back in New Zealand, but his replies were discouraging. He reckoned that his preliminary investigations showed it would cost about 40 grand per person, probably a lot more, once he'd looked into it more deeply. It very much appeared, he wrote, that it might all be too hard.

Dave reckoned it was time for us to organise and do it ourselves. Organising and running commercial trips for large groups and looking after the likes of us, 24-seven, for large chunks of the year, didn't leave Mike Ferris much time or energy for putting together something on the scale of the proposed Silk Road adventure. When we told him we were going to put it all together ourselves, he wished us well in shouldering the burden of what was clearly going to be a major undertaking.

Undaunted, we leapt into it. Dave was all for going then and there. Hang on, we said. We've still got a daughter at home. We wouldn't be able to do anything until Ruby moved out. That meant the earliest we could go was February 2005.

We still knew next to nothing about the Silk Road, beyond what Mike had told us around the campfire that night in the Himalaya. Gareth Googled it, and picked up a bit from the internet; Jo found a copy of the 1958 National Classics Art Type edition of *The Travels of Marco Polo* at a second-hand bookshop one day. Gareth read it, and fell in love with it — with the writing and, of course, with the story. He finished it, and promptly began reading it again. Meanwhile, we plotted the line of the great explorer's route on our old school atlas, from Venice to Beijing.

Hell, we thought, that's a long way.

But seeing this journey set down on paper gave us a starting-point. It would be pretty cool, we both felt, to step (metaphorically speaking) in Marco's 750-year-old footprints.

Economist to the last, the first step Gareth took in planning the trip was raising a spreadsheet. This is how he's done every tour he's ever organised, no matter how long or short. The trip is broken down into stages according to the distances it is feasible to cover in a day's easy riding, worked out by referring to the logbooks of our other trips and determining the average distances we were clocking up in a day's ride in tough country. The idea is to allow plenty of time to get where you want to go by mid-afternoon, with lots of stops along the way. Consulting a map, each night's accommodation is planned and entered into the spreadsheet. Given the scale of this trip, Jo thought it would be sensible to base calculations on a pattern of two days' riding and one day off, to allow for the inevitable problems and delays but also just to prevent it becoming a gruelling ordeal. So that was the basis upon which the trip was planned.

Just how different this enterprise was going to be from your three-week cappuccino canter through, say, the South Island became obvious as the spreadsheet grew. And just how ignorant of contemporary geography we were rapidly came home to us. We knew there were a whole bunch of 'stans in the part of the world the Silk Road traversed, but as we read their names on the map — Turkmenistan, Uzbekistan, Kyrgyzstan — we scratched our heads. We'd never even heard of half these countries; what would it take to be allowed to enter them? What would it be like to travel through them?

We did as much research as we could, from books, the internet and asking anyone we knew or heard of who had travelled in the regions we were proposing to visit, to find out about the countries along the route. Our actual path was a moveable feast. Time and other considerations made it impractical to follow Marco absolutely everywhere: we couldn't go to Iraq, for obvious reasons, and there was no way we were going to be able to make it to the bottom of Iran if Gareth wanted to fulfil a long-standing ambition to visit the Aral Sea, which he'd heard a lot about.

The more we learned, the more we tinkered. For a while there, we weren't going to go to Iran at all. The route we originally plotted would have taken us around the northern end of the Caspian Sea, missing Iran altogether. You don't really hear about Iran as an attractive place to visit: they're building atomic bombs there, you're given to understand, and it's full of ayatollahs and scary Islamic extremists. And given how big it was, it seemed a good spot to drop from the itinerary.

Jo, however, was talking one day to a friend who had actually been there rather than merely read about it in the newspapers: a Japanese woman who is married to a Pakistani. She said: 'You can't *not* go to Iran. You *have* to go to Iran.' At the same time, Gareth was reading about the ferries we were planning to take across the Caspian Sea. There were only two boats in the service, he learned: one of them had just sunk, and the other one completed, on average, only one in five of its scheduled sailings. People regularly boarded for the journey and waited out 72-hour delays, he read, and then when they reached the other end of the trip, they were extorted by Turkmen Customs officials. Suddenly, Iran seemed like an attractive destination.

Another useful source of information for us was the few but very informative motorcycle blogs on the internet. You could enter the name of the country you fancied visiting into these sites and they'd come up with first-hand accounts of people who'd been there, done that by bike. You learned about everything, from what fuel quality and availability were like to the kinds of accommodation available and the more obscure local customs. They were a great help in the planning stages.

We also invited people around to our house for meetings — anyone who we thought might be useful. We had Wellingtonians Lloyd and Julie Powell and David May, who had done much of the journey they would later describe in the book *What The Hell Are We Doing Here?*, based on their experiences flogging Land Rovers through Africa. They came around for dinner and regaled us until the wee hours about the trials and tribulations of their trip. It was very entertaining, and very informative. They had also been to Mongolia, and this section of their trip was directly relevant to us; but their general advice on the practicalities of this kind of expedition to the more rugged parts of the world — border crossings, communicating with people with whom you had barely a word in common, health and safety precautions — was all worth hearing. We soaked it up.

One of the most improbable sources of information we came by was literally almost by accident — an accident that we nearly caused. We were strolling along Victoria Street one day, probably talking about the Silk Road — it occupied most of our thoughts and plenty of our dreams by this stage — when we heard a bike approaching. Like all bikers, we can't not look when a bike goes by. We saw a young man in battered leathers tooling along the road on a bike loaded down with packs and panniers. He had to be a motorcycle tourist. There was no consultation, and neither of us gave it a moment's thought, but next thing we were both leaping out into his path, waving our arms wildly. God knows what he made of us — the mad pedestrians of New Zealand probably joined the rabid dogs of Peru as hazards to the motorcyclist minding his own business for a moment there.

He stopped — he had to — and as he manoeuvred his bike to the side of the road and took off his helmet, we were already firing questions at him. He answered in English heavily accented with German. Yes, he confirmed, he was indeed on a world tour by bike. Yes, he would be happy to accept a coffee and answer our questions. Dinner and a bed for the night? Why yes, he would be delighted.

Ulbrecht proved a mine of information. We ended up giving him a key to our house — something to do with the community of bikers everywhere. We'd been at the receiving end of the same fellow-feeling in the past, and had no hesitation extending it now.

A little later we had a call from Dave in Tauranga.

'You'll never guess who I've just run into,' he said.

It was true: we would never have guessed it. Like us, he had leapt into the path of a grizzled-looking motorcyclist tootling along in Tauranga only to discover that he was none other than the proprietor of the motel where we were considering staying in Naryn, in Kyrgyzstan. Crazy stuff, but once you're in the planning stages of something like this, these little synchronicities just seem to come along.

Items on the television news that would previously have passed us by suddenly assumed a new significance. Any mention of a country whose name ended in -stan, or talk of Turkey, or Kurds, or difficulties in China . . . our ears pricked up. As we were planning the trip, trouble seemed to flare in one 'stan after another. And no sooner would an item screen on the news than the phone would ring. It would be Gareth's mother.

'You're not going to Turkmenistan, are you? It's too dangerous to go there.'

'Yep,' Gareth would reply, just to wind her up. 'We're going straight up the guts.'

As the route began to take shape in theory, we needed to get in touch with someone who had the expertise to put it into practice. Gareth was Googling the Silk Road when he noticed that there was an outfit named Silk Road Adventures, who claimed they could arrange everything necessary for groups wishing to do all or part of it. They sounded useful, particularly for organising the documentation necessary to cross the borders of the 15 countries the route would traverse.

He wondered where they were based, and was a little startled to see that their world headquarters seemed to be located in Greymouth.

Sure enough, when he phoned Murray Reedy, who runs the business with his wife Pat, he learned that Silk Road Adventures was the fruit of a long association between the Kiwi couple and the ancient trading route. Murray readily agreed to lend a hand in the organisation of our adventure. Gareth emailed through the spreadsheet and a few days later a fat package arrived in his letterbox. It was an itinerary prepared by Silk Road Adventures.

A lot of effort had gone into assembling it. Everything was organised, from where we would stay to what we would eat and what we would look at and when. Silk Road Adventures could provide everything. Gareth was appalled.

He phoned Murray.

'What's all this?' he fumed. 'We're bikers. We don't want anyone bloody holding our hands. We want to be independent. That's what biking's all about.'

Murray listened, then explained that it's all very well being independent, but many of the countries we proposed to enter — the former Soviet Central Asian republics, notably, and Iran and China — would not admit us unless our stay was planned to the last detail and executed precisely according to the plan. Gareth grumbled for a while but, asking around, found Murray's account was pretty much universally corroborated. Organisation may be anathema to your average touring biker, but there was no getting around its necessity in the parts of the world we intended to visit.

While we were fine-tuning the itinerary, we put the word out among our biker mates about what we were planning and when, in an effort to recruit the group we had already come to refer to as the Silk Riders. And we had begun to think about the gear we'd need to take along.

Somewhere in the middle stages of our planning, someone — perhaps it was our mate Mike O'Donnell (universally known as 'MoD') — said to Gareth, 'You should get sponsorship, man.'

'What?' Gareth scoffed. 'It's a holiday! You don't get people to sponsor you on holiday!'

But MoD persisted. This, he argued, was a big deal. Everyone who went along would be riding identical bikes for simplicity's sake when it came to maintenance and to carrying spares. Flogging six identical bikes over 18,000 km, in all imaginable conditions, is the kind of product-testing regime most motorcycle manufacturers dream of setting up but can't afford. So why not offer them the chance to participate?

It so happened that Mike had a PowerPoint presentation on file that he had used to try to get Harley-Davidson to sponsor the annual New Zealand Harley rally in Wellington. He pulled it out and, using this as a base, he and Gareth knocked together a proposal. We would offer three tiers of involvement. For a certain sum, a corporate could have naming rights for the venture and the website on which we planned to run updates of our progress. Or they could choose to be a major sponsor, or a minor sponsor.

At that stage, we were tossing up between two bike models: the BMW F650 Dakar or the Yamaha XT. To create some competitive tension, it was decided to target both manufacturers: BMW Motorad and Yamaha.

Our preference was probably BMW. Gareth contacted Geoff Fletcher, the managing director of BMW New Zealand whom he knew slightly as they had once engaged Gareth's consultancy, Infometrics. He was encouraging. 'Yep,' he said, 'there could be mileage in that for us.'

Brendan Keogh, who was BMW's Wellington rep, was enthusiastic about the notion of sponsorship. He arranged to meet us at the company's New Zealand HQ in Auckland. In retrospect, he must have been preparing the ground for us. MoD and Gareth walked into the meeting and did their bit, and the mood was positive. Over the course of the next few weeks, BMW wrote down what they expected to get out of any putative arrangement, and what they were prepared to offer. It looked pretty good to us.

Artfully concealing our disbelief that we had pulled it off, we accepted their terms, and presently received a letter confirming the deal. BMW would sponsor us by providing five brand-new F650 Dakar bikes at a substantial discount, and an F650 GS — a lower bike, on lower suspension with 19-inch front wheels rather than the Dakar's 21-inch — for Jo's shorter legs. Best of all, they reckoned it would be best if we began the ride from the BMW factory in Munich, where the bikes would be tuned, serviced and made ready to go.

Well, that was a pretty successful fishing expedition. If it worked once, Gareth reasoned, why, it might work again. A list of gear was drawn up — a wish-list.

BMW came to the party again with riding gear for all of us, including their excellent Savanna and Rallye riding suits, Rallye GS and Pro winter gloves, Gore-Tex-lined Savanna and Contour boots, and light-yet-strong BMW System 4 flip-face helmets.

The next item on the list was communications gear. Gareth suddenly remembered getting a call a few months earlier from someone at Vodafone who, predictably enough, wanted to complain to him about anti-competitive behaviour by Telecom and enlist his help in exposing it. At the time, Gareth listlessly took down his details, even though he wasn't much interested in getting involved in squabbles between telcos. Then the Silk Road came along. The piece of paper with Andrew Bonica's details was dusted off, and the lines of communication were re-opened. Vodafone, too, were keen to come on board. They supplied nifty little gadgets called i-mates, which have multiple functions in a small, portable package — a phone with voice, text and picture messaging, but also email and a digital camera. With the fold-up keyboard and extra memory-storage cards that Gareth took along, he was able to dispense with the need for a laptop and still run word-processing and spreadsheet software, and use email and the internet. We also took along an Iridium satellite phone.

Now we were on a roll, especially MoD. He just happened to know the head of outdoor equipment manufacturer Fairydown. A couple of phone calls were made, and suddenly we had all our tents, sleeping bags and assorted other items. Meanwhile, Gareth was talking to international aid agency UNICEF, of which he was a trustee. The Silk Road expedition seemed like a golden opportunity to give some publicity to a humanitarian project. UNICEF is perceived to be kind of abstract in the sort of work it does: few people can point to a specific project that they know to be a beneficiary of UNICEF assistance. Gareth was keen to change all that. He offered to use the Silk Road expedition to sponsor UNICEF, but only so long as they nominated a particular target project. UNICEF agreed, and five potential projects along the route were identified. In the end, a village education enterprise in Kyrgyzstan got the nod. As a quid pro quo, UNICEF offered to help us where they could. It turned out they had a close relationship with Lufthansa. Again, phone calls and emails were exchanged, and while Lufthansa don't fly out of New Zealand, they agreed to help wherever practical. Of course, we craftily constructed our itinerary so as to maximise Lufthansa's involvement.

When we did our trip to Nepal, we had cheekily (as we thought then) contacted Jeremy Moon, the founder of merino-clothing supplier Icebreaker, and told him what we proposed to do. He told us that if we could promise to take photographs featuring people wearing Icebreaker clothing while being intrepid in Nepal, he'd supply us with a jacket each. Done! So we naturally went back to him for the Silk Road trip. He was pretty happy with the pictures we got for him in Nepal, so he was willing to help us out on the Silk Road, too. He couldn't give us all the gear free, he told us, but we could have it at wholesale prices.

By now, we were all having a go at it. Jo approached Marvelox in Christchurch and came away with discounted Packsafe security devices for our luggage. Through his business contacts, our friendly BMW rep Brendan Keogh, who had joined the group by this time, lined up Metzeler Tourance tyres for our bikes. The local supplier of Scottoiler automatic chain-oilers kitted us out with these invaluable devices. We worked our way down through the list. Touratech and Givi panniers, check. Water purifiers, check. Ventura headlight guards, check . . .

The funny thing was, when we first circulated the group to tell them about the sponsored gear we had lined up, a couple of them were stand-offish. Sponsorship sounded like something that might come with strings attached, you see: commitment, obligations — anathema to a free spirit like a biker. They were a bit the same about our involvement with UNICEF — 'I won't have to do any publicity, will I?' was their question — but their resistance collapsed once free or cheap biking gear was waved in front of them. There were dark mutterings when the possibility of a film crew catching up with us en route was mooted but, happily, that fell through. In the end, when Jo sent out the Icebreaker catalogue to see what everyone wanted, it was our two recalcitrant Silk Riders who placed the biggest orders.

Shaping up and shaking down

From the moment we decided the Silk Road was a goer, we began to turn our minds to the other great mystery factor of the trip: who was going to come with us? Needless to say, this was going to be a little bit different from a day trip that begins and ends in your garage. It was going to be expensive. It was going to require three months out of your life. It was going to be trying, and almost certainly dangerous at times. We couldn't count upon any outside assistance. There would be no permanent support vehicle or professional guide along on this trip. We needed to ensure that between the members of the group, we covered the range of skills we would need to get ourselves out of the poo. And, just as important, we would have to get along.

That last one, of course, was the hard bit. To start with, everyone we took along was going to be a biker. That meant they would have a character flaw in common: they would be, as all bikers are, individualistic to the point of sheer, bloody-minded arrogance. Second, there would be competitive issues to deal with. Biking is a testosterone-fuelled activity. It needn't be, but it just seems to lend itself to it. Shove all that chrome, metallic paint and rumbling power between a man's legs and it's bound to give him ideas about himself. Every trip we've ever been on has had its moments through the stupid rivalries that arise from lads trying to outdo one another. Or worse, trying to outdo Jo. At the start of every single trip, there's always someone who tries to cut her off on a corner, or passes her on a straight, to try to show her who wears the leather biking pants. At these times, Gareth usually groans, 'Here we go' and, sure enough, it's all on. It's pretty rare for her to lose these contests. She may not have the testosterone, but she's got the rugged individualism, complete with the competitive edge, in spades. That said, the worst thing you can do is be chivalrous to her. Make way for her, or in any way imply she needs special treatment, and look out. Plenty of our trips have had these moments, too.

The other curious factor that arises from having Jo along is the difficulty some of our touring companions have had with us being a couple. When we've been away for a couple of weeks, some of the boys start missing their own partners. Others aren't by themselves by choice. Either way, the slightest show of conjugal bliss seems to cause great resentment. Many's the time we've emerged from our tent and been greeted by grim faces.

'I've been chasing bloody sheep all night,' someone will warn. 'You even smile . . . !'

We try to avoid anything that might inflame this kind of situation. There's no gazing into one another's eyes, cracking cosy little in-jokes, holding hands or anything like that.

So these were some of the considerations.

From the earliest planning stages, we began talking about the Silk Road trip with our motorcycling mates when we were out touring, and people began putting their hands up to come along. Starry-eyed optimism pretty quickly gave way for most as they began to work out where the money, the time and the spousal permission would come from. Most who were dead certain they'd be there at the start line fell by the wayside.

One who didn't was 'Captain' Bryan Wyness, a 63-year-old former airline pilot and Air New Zealand senior manager. Another was Phil 'the Sea Lord' Lough, the 57-year-old chairman of the New Zealand Trade and Enterprise board, a director of assorted other companies and former CEO of Sealord. Both ride with Gareth's touring group. Even so, Phil couldn't quite spare the time to do the whole trip, so it was decided to offer Phil a 'Half Marco', which would see him take a bike to the midway point of the trip — somewhere in Uzbekistan, if our maths was right — and surrender it there to another rider, who would take it the rest of the way. Selwyn Blinkhorne, a 56-year-old Wellington financial analyst and another riding companion (he had done two of our previous trips, to the Himalaya and the Andes), said he would take the other 'Half-Marco'. Our old riding buddy, 37-year-old communications manager and new father Mike 'MoD' O'Donnell, was keen to come along. Along with Gareth and Jo and Dave Wallace, that was seven.

One day, while the decision about which kind of bikes we would use on the trip was still up in the air, Dave and Jo were in Motorad Ltd, the Wellington BMW dealership, checking out the Dakar. Jo was sitting astride one, and shaking her head at Dave.

'Too high. Can't get my feet down on this,' she was saying.

The shop's owner, 52-year-old Brendan Keogh, approached, and asked what she needed the bike for.

They told him. He raised his eyebrows, then quizzed them about the detail of the plan, listening intently.

'I'd be keen on that,' he said at the end of the conversation. 'I'd like to come along.'

'OK, great,' said Jo. 'You're in.'

They swapped details. As they walked out of the shop, Dave said to Jo, 'How long have you known him for?'

Jo counted back.

'About three minutes,' she replied. 'About as long as you have.'

Dave looked dubious.

'Don't worry about it,' Jo said. 'Everyone says they want to come along, but they all fade when push comes to shove.'

Well, as it turned out, Brendan was a little harder to shake loose than all that. That made eight.

When you put together an expedition like the one we were proposing to tackle, everybody has to bring something to the table — to take responsibility for some aspect of the organisation, whether it be logistical, medical, mechanical or maintenance.

Our group of seven seemed to offer a nice, complementary range of skills. Bryan, Brendan and Dave were all fix-it men; Bryan and Brendan are bloody good on the mechanical side of things and Dave — a typical cocky — is just great at coming up with good, practical solutions to problems. Bryan is just one of the nicest blokes you'd hope to have along on a trip, always positive and cheerful, and meticulous about organisation. Brendan, a former New Zealand Enduro dirt-bike champion, is one of the best off-road riders in the country, and would be invaluable in coaching us in the finer points of technique when necessary. Phil is a great manager of personalities and a clear-thinking problem-solver.

All of us — especially Phil, of course — were grateful that Selwyn was keen to take over Phil's bike at the halfway point, and we had no real reservations about his ability to fit in and contribute. He's a biker mate of ours of fairly long standing, and very competent on his machine. The challenge for Selwyn, as we all knew, would be breaking into the group after we'd all been on the road for weeks, ironing out those kinks in group dynamics that inevitably occur.

Jo, with no nursing qualifications but a couple of St John's courses under her belt, volunteered to handle the medical side of things. Added to that, she's an extrovert, and a bit of a diplomat — qualities that Gareth couldn't be said to have in abundance. But Gareth, of course, was born to lead.

Not far into the 18 months or so the eight of us spent planning the trip intensively, it became clear that MoD, who would dearly have loved to come, just couldn't afford the time. He was going to have to drop out, but he remained deeply involved. It was a tragedy that MoD was unavailable, because he is one of our great mates, hugely respected in motorcycling circles and pretty knowledgeable about everything to do with Beamers and the BMW organisation.

Early on we got around the table at Gareth and Jo's house and discussed all aspects of the trip, dividing up the tasks according to our particular skill-base and set of contacts. We ran it like a business, with action plans, designated areas of competence and responsibility, cut-off dates, the works. Whenever we thought we might be getting a little bit carried away with it all, we just looked at the atlas. The scale of the undertaking continually reassured us that our fanatical attention to detail was warranted. This was a major enterprise.

You could put together the most compatible, complementary, multiskilled set of riders in the world and your trip could still turn pear-shaped if you didn't pay attention to the quality that, above all else, distinguishes expedition riders from the various other species of biker. Expedition riding is, in the end, a team sport, and your riders have to be team players. In other words, on the road, each must always be looking out for the welfare of the others. The reason is obvious. An expedition ride is long, covering several months, and not infrequently a number of countries; everyone along probably wants slightly different things out of it. But everyone has one goal in common, and that is to get everyone to the end. If one bike goes down, preventing its rider from completing, then the expedition has failed. So you've got to ensure there's a system in place amongst the group for members to lend a helping hand to anyone who strikes trouble.

What's more, if a rider or machine is taken out, everyone is held up while repairs are made so that the trip can continue. Unlike on a normal tour, you can't just call up the local dealer to fix the bike, or send the rider to the nearest hospital and continue on. So the more quickly support from other team members gets there, the more quickly the trip can resume.

For these reasons, an expedition ride really only works if each member takes responsibility for the one behind them, making sure they are continually in touch with that rider. The rider in front of you is pretty much irrelevant, so long as they're upright; it's the one behind that matters. This way, when a bike stops with a problem, before long all bikes have regrouped at that spot and the full skill-set of the group is at hand to solve the problem.

All it takes for the team to be compromised is for a single rider to ignore that simple rule, and cruise along looking out only for number one. Others may try to compensate, but this approach is a distant second-best. Long delays and huge double-backs to trouble spots will inevitably ensue.

As a chain is only as strong as its weakest link, an expedition team's on-the-road efficiency is constrained by the reliability of its weakest member. A single unreliable individual can almost double your travelling time, because you never know whether it's the guy behind you who is the unreliable one, so you should therefore be ignoring him and looking out for the second rider back.

That is the basis of rider etiquette, and it was one of the major items in a two-page document entitled 'Rules of the Road' which Gareth and Dave presented to each member of the team. There was a bit of mirth, a bit of indignation at it — Gareth was assured he was anally retentive and should seek help — but as they read through it, most of the boys saw its value. After all, as the document itself pointed out, if we didn't get everyone to buy in at the outset, the trip might be conducted — heaven forbid — democratically, and then where would we be? Far better, we decided, to establish a consultative dictatorship and stick to it.

Some of the items probably seemed like common sense. Everyone should make sure they were up to the trip, physically and financially, because the collapse of either your health or your means would be as catastrophic for the group's prospects as a mechanical breakdown. We all had inoculations against the various nasties we might succumb to along the route, including such exotic and fabulous-sounding diseases as rabies, and while Jo was to be our resident medico, we all did first-aid refresher courses, and learned such useful tricks as how to amputate a limb, or how to dress a gunshot wound under field conditions (stick a tampon in the hole).

The document emphasised that we were travelling together, and we must therefore stick together. People could divert from the route collectively taken but only if it was collectively agreed, and we would always all stay at the same place unless there were some *force majeure* preventing it. And rider etiquette — the art of riding as a team — would apply at all times.

The bikes arrived in August 2004, which was an exciting time for all of us. It was a bit like an early Christmas. They needed to be set up with the frames for the panniers and suchlike, and then we needed to run them in, riding them easy for the first 1000 km or so. They were great to ride. Most bikes encourage you into one of two riding postures. The Ducati that Jo generally rides in New Zealand, for example, requires you to adopt the 'sport position' — bum up, head down — which is pretty hard on the wrists and not much good for sightseeing. Gareth's Harley-Davidson, on the other hand, makes you sit back with your feet forward and your arms high. In this position, your chest is presented to the full force of the wind, and riding like this over long distances is really hard on your back. The upright position of the Dakar, by contrast, is brilliant for sightseeing, because you look around yourself like a meerkat. It's not so hard on your back or wrists and the front fairing deflects the wind up and over you.

We quickly realised they're quite light, which is a good thing off-road, particularly if you put one down — which is one of those quaint bits of biker-speak for falling off. On the road, however, they tend to get blown around a bit if there's any kind of cross-breeze. While they are hardly rocket-ships — you have to really wind them up to go over 120 km/h — they cruise at between 90 and 110 km/h very nicely indeed. All in all, they seemed to represent a good compromise between on- and off-road configurations, and were ideal for our purposes.

In the initial planning, we looked at some of the options. Dave and Gareth decided to go for Staintune exhaust systems (supplied by a mate of Dave's, Tony Rees Motorcycles in Whakatane), and they also explored the possibility of fitting long-range tanks. In fact, they went so far as to order these. By the time they arrived, however, Gareth had decided that there was no problem with the availability of fuel along the route: issues were more likely to arise with fuel quality. He decided he could get by strapping four 2 litre jerry cans to the bike. Dave, meanwhile, thought it would be a good idea if at least one bike in the group had extra range, and set about trying to convert his bike to a supertanker. There can't be many better bike mechanics around than Dave, but he was buggered if he could make the thing fit. After spending hours on it, he gave it away and ended up on a bike with no additional fuel capacity. Jo didn't carry any auxiliary cans either. As it transpired, we never had problems getting fuel.

You never really know how a touring group is going to function till you've been riding together. It's impossible to predict how personalities and relationships are going to cope with the peculiar stresses and strains imposed by touring conditions. And until everyone knows everyone else's capabilities and competencies, both on the bikes and off, you don't really know how the group is going to fit together. At the outset of every trip we've ever been on, unless it was with people we know really well, there's always been a kind of jostling to establish a pecking order. We've seen some spectacular tantrums. You don't want to be going through that nonsense at the beginning of a trip like the Silk Road. Imagine discovering two days into a three-month tour that you can't stand half the group you're with, or that certain members can't cope, or won't observe riding etiquette.

So it was important to mount some kind of shakedown expedition. To ensure that there was a dose of hardship involved — the acid test — we decided to head for outback Australia. We told everyone it was to try out the bikes, but it was really to try out one another. Probably everyone knew this; certainly, if they had any sense, they would have been as anxious as we were to suss everybody else out.

The plan for the Australian assault was to take the bikes across in time to catch the 2004 Australian Motorcycle Grand Prix at the world-famous Phillip Island circuit, and then to head around the Lucky Country's harsh Red Centre. Of the Silkies, Gareth, Dave, Phil, Bryan and MoD were along for the ride. Also there were Brent Fergusson, Pete Larsen and Mark and Miriam Holloway. Everyone was riding Dakars apart from MoD, who was on a big Beamer, an 1150GS, and Mark and Miriam who, against everyone's better judgement, were tackling the trip two-up on a Harley-Davidson 1450 Road King.

As it was Ruby's last few months at home, Jo decided to stay at home and look after her. She helped with the organisation and the preparations for the trip and saw Gareth off at the airport. But after a couple of quiet days at home, she thought to herself, this is ridiculous.

Son Floyd was at home: he could look after Ruby. So Jo packed up her own bike and took off upcountry to Lake Waikaremoana, in order to get a bit of gravel time under her own belt.

All the other bikes were packed in a container and shipped to Melbourne in September; we flew over and picked them up on October 15. We enjoyed the grand prix, but the ride home from Phillip Island way overshadowed it, as we did it in the company of over 15,000 other bikes. The most memorable moment in the day for Gareth was when Bryan cruised into the forecourt of a service station and clipped a bike. It fell over, collecting the next which, in accordance with classical domino-effect theory, toppled into the next, and the next, and so on, until about ten bikes were lying on the deck. Their owners were inside paying. Bryan was gazing in bemusement at the havoc he'd wreaked when Dave pulled in.

'For Christ's sake pick your bike up!' he hissed. 'Look at the bike you've just knocked over. What kind of dude d'you reckon rides that? And what d'you reckon he'll do when he comes out?'

Suddenly, Bryan's need for gas wasn't so pressing.

From Melbourne, we made our way south via the lovely, mellow country of Victoria and South Australia, collecting a speeding ticket and some useful route advice on the way from a couple of undercover policemen dressed as surfies who clocked Gareth and MoD being naughty on the smooth straights and beautifully cambered curves of the Great Ocean Highway. The adventure proper began at Port Augusta, about six hours north of Adelaide, from which they started the infamous Birdsville Track, which heads due north towards the former nuclear facility at Woomera. The land quickly grew more desolate with the temperature sitting around 35 degrees Celsius. At Lyndhurst the rough asphalt gave way to red dirt. That was the last we'd see of sealed roads for 3000 km. From here on in, it was just a matter of picking your line and keeping an eye out for the emus that occasionally darted across the road.

After a couple of hours running on passable tracks, things changed as we reached the fringes of the Simpson Desert. We found ourselves in gravel — drifts of marble-sized, rolling stones that the locals call 'gibba'. It was like riding in a pile of ball bearings. The bikes slewed left and right as everyone fought to negotiate it. Phil, who had little off-road riding experience, was finding it hard going.

'Ignore the track in front of you,' Dave told him. 'Focus on the horizon and keep your body vertical. If you feel yourself going over then gun the bike and the power will make her stand up.'

Counterintuitive as it seems, that was the right approach — the wobblier you felt, the more power you applied — and it seemed to work.

That night was spent at the Mungerannie Roadhouse. The roadhouse was pretty typical of the settlements we visited over the course of the next week: your first impression is a lurch of disappointment when this clutch of dilapidated, prefab buildings hoves in view, but this is quickly dispelled as soon as you open the door and find yourself in a wonderful, air-conditioned oasis.

The next day we continued 400 km up the Birdsville Track to the town that gives it its name. The route consisted of three roughly equal sections — gibba, rutted clays and shingle — all good practice, if you were in the mood for accentuating the positive. At the end of the long, long day, it was hard for any of us to form an objective view of Birdsville, so welcome was the sight of it. There, we set up the bikes for the even harder days to come. Each bike was loaded up with enough extra fuel to get us back from the theoretical point of no return, along with 6 litres of water per person per day. We canvassed the locals' opinions on the venture, and these ranged from 'No worries' to 'You're bloody mad. Two bikers died on that track last year.'

The group left just before sunrise and made slow progress, unwilling to go any faster than 30 km/h for fear of collecting kangaroos. By eight in the morning, the temperature was already pushing 40 degrees Celsius as we entered the Cordillo Downs Track which would take us through the Sturt Stony Desert. Riding etiquette is vital in such circumstances. Everyone was supposed to take responsibility for the rider behind them: from time to time when they didn't, tempers flared.

Around midday the gibba gave way to knuckle-sized rocks and Mark and Miriam took their first dive. After all, the Harley is called a Road King, not a Gravel King, or Sand Dune King. It was right out of its natural habitat and overloaded to hell. It took all hands to heave the heavy hog — we reckoned it must have weighed over a tonne with all its gear aboard — upright again. The crash had cracked the exhaust and the kickstand, but rider and passenger were only lightly bruised. Once they were pumped up with electrolyte solution, everyone continued, albeit more slowly.

Even when we reached the 'main' shingle road we found that a spell of high winds had reduced it to a set of sand dunes with a v-shaped track winding through the middle. The easier going that everyone had been anticipating was clearly not going to materialise. Everyone contemplated this fact in silence, broken only by the odd profanity. Phil, who was struggling with the heat and painful wrists, took it particularly hard.

There was no option but to press on, so everyone got into sand-plough mode. We were all dehydrating fast — sweating it out, but also leaking from the main seal, as we were all suffering diarrhoea at this point. Everyone was experiencing sand flops, and the effort required to heave the bikes upright in the soft sand, particularly the Harley, taxed us all to the limit. Some bloody holiday.

It took over two hours to traverse the 40 km of dune, then we finally struck something approaching a negotiable track. All the same, it took another gruelling four hours of riding before we reached Innamincka, just after sunset. Half the group had to be practically carried indoors from their bikes, such was their state of exhaustion.

The next day promised easier going, as we began the Strzelecki Track, but our hopes were soon cruelly dashed. The ubiquitous red sand had again invaded the way forward, and muscles aching from the day before strained to keep riders upright. Then the Harley hit trouble on its way up a deeply rutted hill. Just before the top, it backfired violently and died. The cause was easily determined: the battery was cracked right through, killing the electrics and the fuel injection stone dead.

This is a bad thing at the best of times, but when you're 80 km from the nearest living soul, it can hardly be called the best of times. Mark refused to leave the bike, so Gareth — perhaps out of the goodness of his fellow Harley-owner's heart — stayed with him while the rest rode 80 hellish kilometres to the next piece of civilisation. Here, a saintly farmer's wife used her 4WD and a trailer to get everyone and the dethroned Road King to Cameron's Corner, the hot, dusty, godforsaken meeting-place of Queensland, South Australia and New South Wales.

At dawn the next day, Dave rode 180 km to Tibooburra, the nearest place where we could hope to get a battery. His return journey nearly ended when a suicidal dingo cut across his path, nearly tipping him off. Then the party set out again. The Harley had all but had it by now, and it commenced self-dismantling. One split pannier started depositing undies, like some kind of distress signal, all the way along the track, eventually falling off altogether. The exhaust headers flexed and cracked, with neither Mark nor Miriam any the wiser. They were a sorry sight hauling into Tibooburra, towing their remaining (now empty) pannier several feet behind them, by a single bungee cord. Miriam collapsed with sunstroke and had to be admitted to hospital. Some holiday indeed!

As Miriam was re-hydrated and cooled down, our resident Harley expert, Captain Bryan, descended on the hapless machine and, with the universal tools of wire, gaffer tape and Loctite, attempted some sort of rebuild. The rest of the boys scoured the desert for Mark's possessions, aided by a kilometres-long trail of blue men's underpants, spaced exactly 100 metres apart. They managed to locate every item.

The next day, the group pushed south to Broken Hill and re-encountered civilisation. The novelty of cellphones, running water and sealed roads turned us into a bunch of moist-eyed, foolishly grinning idiots. Further and more sophisticated repairs were effected upon the Harley, and we began our return to Melbourne.

Several relatively uneventful days later, as we packed the bikes into the container for their journey home, we agreed we'd been lucky. The outback is no place for poor preparation nor, as had been demonstrated, Road Kings. On the other hand, it was the best possible field test for the Dakars and touring gear we intended to take on the Silk Road. And we learned plenty about the group, as well. Talking it over with Dave, we decided we were a trifle anxious about Phil. He was pretty inexperienced on the terrain that lay waiting in Central Asia — the trip to Aus had been his first off-road venture, a veritable baptism of fire, and he had struggled. He'd also suffered badly from the heat, which was not a great sign, given we intended crossing some of the world's great deserts. And it hadn't escaped Gareth and Dave's attention that Brent had looked after Phil all the way round. They're great mates, and when they're together on tour as thick as thieves. We weren't sure we could afford that kind of situation on the Silk Road. On the other hand, Brent wasn't going. But he did take Jo aside before we left and made her promise to look after his mate, a need that in the event never really arose.

After Australia, doubts were raised about Dave, too. He has an abrupt, occasionally abrasive manner, and is not one of the world's great communicators. He's a farmer, after all. It's easy to read him wrong, particularly if you're from the CBD. Jo, for example, got off on the wrong foot with him: he tends to pepper his speech with profanities, and soon after they'd met, referred to her as 'camp bitch'. She took exception.

'See?' Dave's wife, Yvonne, said to him. 'Nice people don't call each other things like "camp bitch".'

Dave seemed genuinely surprised.

Several of the boys took Gareth aside after Australia and told him it would be madness to give Dave any kind of leadership role on the Silk Road. But neither Gareth nor Jo had any fears whatsoever where Dave was concerned. Get past the rough exterior, and you'll find him utterly reliable, competent, self-reliant, and yet completely selfless with it. The communication issue was a minor problem beside the qualities he offered and, in the end, it was all a matter of adjustment. When Dave is addressing you, Jo reckoned, the trick was to think of yourself as a much-loved sheepdog.

By Christmas 2004, everything was pretty much in place. We had our route sorted out, we had our group, and we'd even reconciled the two. The main sticking point in this regard had been Phil, who had lived in Iran for three years when he'd worked for the New Zealand Dairy Board. When he learned we proposed to pass through Iran, he became unhappy.

It turned out that several of the Iranians he had dealt with in his time there were now dead, killed in the Islamic Revolution. We also learned that his daughter was born there, and when his term was up, the authorities wouldn't let her leave. Phil and his wife, Christine, had to smuggle her out.

Phil just shook his head.

'I'm not going to Iran,' he said.

Even once we'd made it clear it was necessary to go into Iran, he was adamant he wasn't going to Tehran, particularly on a motorbike. The traffic, he reckoned, had to be seen to be believed. In order to get into Turkmenistan, we insisted, we needed to go to the Turkmen embassy, and that meant Tehran. Eventually he gave way, but he clearly wasn't happy.

The first couple of months of 2005 were spent in a fever of excited anticipation, putting the finishing touches to arrangements. We did plenty of publicity in local newspapers and magazines, and jacked up interview schedules for when we were on the ride itself. Our website, which had a map of our route and plenty of descriptive detail about the history and contemporary geography of the areas through which we would pass, was already attracting an enormous amount of attention.

Come February, and it was time for Ruby to leave home. When your last child leaves the nest, it can cause a pretty empty feeling. We were scarcely aware of it: too much else on our minds. Who'd have bikers for parents?

The feeling, however, was mutual. At a dinner we had with the kids just before we left, Jo said to Gareth: 'If anything happens to me and I die over there, promise me you'll just stick me in a hole and carry on. Mark the grave and the kids can do an annual pilgrimage to wherever it is you buried me.'

'Cool,' said one of the kids. 'If you die, we get an overseas trip every year.'

To the start line

We flew to Hong Kong and met up with Dave, who made his way there separately. Phil and Bryan were also already overseas, and due to meet us in Germany. Brendan was busily trying to extricate himself from his business in Wellington. The three of us connected in Hong Kong with a Lufthansa flight to Germany. Our flight path to Frankfurt took us across much of the route we would soon be travelling — across the Tibetan Plateau, the Taklamakan Desert, the Aral and Caspian seas. One obvious feature was the lack of obvious features, just bloody snow everywhere. We took turns pressing our faces to the windows and watching the landscape unroll beneath us: rock, ice, snow and sand, with only the occasional glimpse of anything signifying human habitation. How on earth we expected to cross all this on motorbikes in just a few weeks, none of us quite knew. There was going to have to be a whole lot of thawing going on before we hit it or we were going to be a little 'traction-lite' for the conditions.

The other striking feature, of course, was the scale of it. If we thought we'd got a handle on things sitting at home carving maps into 200-km chunks, the experience of flying over it, hour upon hour, was sobering to say the least. This was no jaunt in the Wairarapa. Not even our Andes or Himalayan adventures rated alongside it.

We were expecting bureaucracy to be one of the major hassles on this trip, but none of us expected to hit it quite as soon as we did. Once we were on the ground in Frankfurt, we learned the good news: our bikes were, as planned, on the docks in Hamburg. Then we learned the bad news: German Customs was 'challenging our legitimacy' and refusing to release them. We tried to establish what shenanigans they thought we were planning, but never got a coherent answer. It appeared, so far as we could gather from the various conversations we had in pidgin English, that there was a problem with our carnets, the bits of paper you need when you're taking goods — the motorcycles and our luggage — across borders.

We spent much of our first four days in Germany shuttling back and forth between the various headquarters of the German and Kiwi bureaucracies to clear up whatever compliance we hadn't fulfilled, bombarding them with documents. It's at times like these you're so grateful for technology. The ether was fairly crackling with our cellphone transmissions, faxes and text messages, as we made the time difference between hemispheres work in our favour. As one lot of apparatchiks slept, we ensured the other lot moved paper; come home-time for them, we turned our attention to filling the working day for their counterparts with as much wheedling and nagging as lay in our power, which was not a little.

We tried everything we could think of. When even BMW couldn't make any headway, things looked pretty hopeless, but under the remorseless barrage, something had to give. After four days of round-the-clock pressure — and Jo's unrelenting vigil to ensure that Gareth didn't point out to the German authorities that it was no wonder they lost the war — the New Zealand Automobile Association was able to prevail upon its German counterpart to enquire of Customs as to what the hell the problem was. Our carnets, we finally learned, were all in order, but applied only to our bikes. They didn't cover our luggage, and this was the sticking point. After a little more to-ing and fro-ing between the German AA and the bureaucrats, and the generation of another small mountain of paper, the latter declared there to be 'no more problems', and permission was given for the container holding the bikes to be uplifted from the wharves and to proceed south to the BMW factory in Munich. There, BMW proposed to give them the once-over and have them all ready for the big day: our departure on the first leg of our trip, south to Venice.

The bikes arrived the day before the rest of the Silk Rider contingent did, and the day before we were scheduled to leave. Had Dave, Jo and Gareth not decided to spend that extra week in Germany, we would have been a week behind schedule before we'd even started, sorting out all the bureaucracy.

The great thing about mobile communications technology is that it freed us up to trip around the place a bit. Not by motorbike, of course, but on the impressive train system. The trains over there go at about 250 km/h — sort of exhilarating and terrifying at the same time. We spent an interesting couple of days in the Czech Republic, as guests of young New Zealander Nigel Stanford, who is surfing the technology wave from the formerly benighted countries of the Soviet bloc. It seems Prague is the latest place to be. It's a party town at the moment, full of very young people doing very young things. Nigel and his mates were busy building websites for international net entities and living a Bohemian lifestyle.

From Prague, we crossed back into the former East Germany and stayed with Heiko, a language student whom we had hosted in Wellington back in the 1990s, around the time the Berlin Wall came down. We had kept in touch, and Heiko reciprocated our hospitality by taking us around the sights. Gareth was particularly keen to get the feel of the not-long liberated society. The East is no way as buoyant as West Germany and as if to confirm this impression, on one of our jaunts we stumbled across a neo-Nazi rally in Eisenach. The shaven-headed, heavy-set demonstrators were expressing political views that made Gareth look like a Fabian socialist. Now *that* was scary.

The integration of East and West Germany after the fall of the Berlin Wall was never going to be easy. The West German economy would probably have had enough on its plate — what with the impact of globalisation — the expansion of the EU, and the soaring euro, without having to find room for 17 million East Germans in the new setup. It's in real trouble, and any progress toward a solution is hampered by the famous German welfare state, which insulates the average German against the worst effects of the slump. The lifestyle of the East Germans appears reasonably affluent, and while many of them still live in Communist-era tenement buildings with all the aesthetic appeal of ablution blocks, you don't see the desperation you might expect in an economy where unemployment is well into the double digits.

Gareth's social commentary on these observations, at any rate, was what his travelling companions had to put up with. The long trip in prospect suddenly seemed a hell of a lot longer!

He had a point when it came to German bureaucracy, however. When we told Heiko of our plight with Customs over unspecified problems with the importation of our motorbikes, he had no hesitation in laying the blame at the door of the bureaucrats. He reckoned they were bound to be gratuitously putting obstacles in our way purely for their own amusement. We were pretty sceptical about all that until one of the officials who assisted in sorting the whole thing out more or less confirmed it. Even when we'd got the carnets corrected, there was no point in getting carried away: the bureaucrats hadn't finished with us yet. We still hadn't received the third-party insurance cards we needed to ride legally on German roads. We learned that the completed insurance forms had been couriered to BMW Munich, but that was as helpful as finding out they'd been sent to a small town in New Zealand — that's how big the corporation is.

Finally, after a week of war with German Customs, and a couple of days frantically getting all our gear organised for the trip (greatly assisted by BMW Motorad Munich, whose technicians spent hours uploading maps and data to our GPS units and sorting out any technical queries we had with the bikes), the big day was upon us. The six of us met up at the hotel the night before we were due to leave.

It usually doesn't take many nights on the road on a bike trip before the group has to come to terms with the agreed ground rules and there's always the odd looming crisis to avert. This trip was no different, except that the need to have those rules in place from the outset was perhaps a little more acute, given how long we were going to be spending in one another's company.

This trip was notable for the fact that we struck one of those shakedown moments before we'd even sat on our bikes. At the restaurant that night, Gareth announced the policy decision we — together with Dave — had arrived at in planning the trip. Unless it was specifically agreed otherwise from time to time, everyone would pay for their own meals. As we'd expected, there was a modest uproar at this. The company directors, retired airline pilots and stockbrokers in our midst scoffed. But of course, this was precisely why we'd decided upon the rule in the first place. We had a long road ahead of us, and a lot of meals to pay for along the way. We wouldn't all want to eat the same food, or drink as much, as everyone else, and we didn't want anyone getting into a situation where they felt they were subsidising the others' tastes or drinking habits. From such petty niggles major upheavals arise.

We also had a snorer in our midst, one whose virtuoso pitch and volume has been known to set Indian villagers running for cover to escape the rogue elephant that they are perfectly certain is rampaging toward them. When he's along on bike tours in New Zealand and we haul into a motorcamp, it's pretty common for everyone else to request tent sites or cabins at the other end of the site from Bryan. Naturally enough, we had to quarantine the offender, but as we had an even number of people, a round of negotations ensued over who would volunteer to be Bryan's room-mate, or who would pay the additional charge for a single rather than a twin hotel room. With a mimimum of acrimony, we struck a formula that promised to satisfy everyone. The guys would rotate the position, so that each in turn could decide whether to endure Bryan's serenade or to pay for single accommodation. We even offered (unsuccessfully!) to play our part, so that Gareth or Jo would take a turn in the roster, so as to keep it all perfectly democratic. So peace reigned in camp — beyond the walls of that single room, at any rate.

All this talk of restaurants and hotel rooms probably makes you wonder what kind of rugged adventure this was. We had tents, sleeping bags and all the rest of the gear necessary for sleeping out under the stars, but while a better class of accommodation was available, all that stuff could stay happily packed away in panniers. We'd be roughing it soon enough. Make hay while the sun still shines was the prevailing feeling.

The day of departure dawned, and Munich obliged us with sunshine and 25 degrees Celsius. To our surprise, we had a farewell party of one to see us off. John Tavener, an English motorcyclist who we had met on the Cook Strait ferry a year earlier, journeyed from Yorkshire to Bavaria to bid us goodbye. For that first day there was a ride of 300 km through two countries in prospect. Life seemed pretty sweet.

As we milled about packing our machines, with BMW staff hovering and taking photographs for the company's in-house magazine, the significance of the moment began to dawn on us. Marco Polo's Silk Road had been nothing more than a dream two years earlier. After all that planning, all those meetings, the emails, faxes, letters, phone calls and the wrangling with bureaucracy, the six of us were standing on European soil with our bikes gassed up and ready to go. There was nothing left now but to 'just do it'. It was pretty moving for all of us, especially the pair of us and Dave, the three who had been in on the adventure from the first.

Loading up the bikes took bloody ages, as it always does, especially when you're really keen to hit the road. There wasn't much science involved, as we had yet to work out what gear would be needed on the road — and what wouldn't and could therefore be stuffed way down near the bottom. With all the gear aboard, the bikes looked more like packhorses than anything else. Once we were organised, we shook hands with the BMW guys, mounted up, turned the keys on our bikes and pressed the buttons. Our six 650 cc steeds fired up and ran sweetly.

Time to go.

About bang-on the departure time we'd scheduled all those months ago, we eased our way out into the traffic. Jo had had the bright idea of tying ribbons to the right handlebar of each bike to help in the process of overcoming all that conditioning which says veer left when traffic trouble arises. Veer left here and you're bang in the path of the oncoming traffic. Our rule in Europe was 'follow the ribbon to the curb'.

We'd planned a route to avoid the autobahn, as we had yet to familiarise ourselves with the way the bikes handled under their loads. How wise this decision was became clear when, after an hour or so of stiff, diffident riding in the Bavarian countryside, it began to bucket down. We stopped, broke out our wet-weather gear and pressed on. Travelling at autobahn speeds would have been too risky, we all agreed: the danger of aquaplaning under sudden braking would have made it pretty hairy. Perhaps it was the conditions, or perhaps it was the daunting prospect of how many miles we had to cover, but there was none of the testosterone-driven bullshit you normally get at the start of one of these trips — none of the racing, the hot-dogging, the territorial overtaking we'd seen on every big trip we'd ever done. They often say the riskiest time on long motorbike journeys is the first few kilometres and the last, and we've seen time and time again how true this is. But we had a pretty good bunch, we knew one another pretty well, and consequently no one felt they had a point to make.

We cruised south in the rain through the lower reaches of Germany and into Austria, to the foothills of the Alps. It was all picture-postcard stuff, everything dressed in spring green and manicured like parkland. One noticeable thing — in the sense it was impossible *not* to notice on a bike — was the smell from the farms. In that part of the world, they keep their livestock indoors in the winter, and when they're mucking out, they just heap up the dung right outside the sheds and byres. Come spring, you've got this mountain of accumulated winter ordure thawing out, and the smell is horrendous. They're used to it, I suppose, but it's a bit of an affront to antipodean olfactory sensibilities. It took Jo to see through to the romantic angle of even the mountains of shit surrounding us: that smell must be indelibly associated with spring in these parts. You get a whiff of that after a long, bitter winter, and your spirits would just rise. It's the stink of warmer weather in prospect.

We stopped at a gas station in Austria, and a crowd of tourists disgorged from their coach and crowded around the astronauts and their heavily laden bikes. They were principally Germans, and as none of us spoke the language, there was more nodding and smiling than actual comprehension going on. But the value of putting a map of our route on the panniers — this was Dave's idea — was obvious,

Above: *Departure day — the Silk Riders pose for photos in Munich before getting on the road. From left: Dave Wallace, Bryan Wyness, Phil Lough, Jo and Gareth Morgan and Brendan Keogh. Inset: Selwyn Blinkhorne.*

Below: *A plaque at the site of Marco Polo's family home in Venice.*

Above: *Silk Riders hang a New Zealand flag from the tower of the house where Marco Polo was born.*

Right: *Balkan bogs — with the doors blown off.*

Below: *Marco Polo's birthplace — Korcula Island, Croatia.*

Above: *The group pays its respects at the Anzac memorial, Gallipoli.*

Below: *A vertically challenged mosque on Turkey's Black Sea coast.*

Above: *Jo, deep in marriage negotiations with Turkish schoolboys.*

Below: *No, not Ruapehu and Ngauruhoe but Mt Ararat and friend, viewed from Iran.*

Above: *Welcome to Iran from a couple of ayatollahs.*

Below: *Girl-talk in Tabriz, Iran.*

Above: *Nice ass!*

Right: *Jo takes a culturally sensitive and compliant dip in the Caspian.*

Below: *A typical Iranian street: women are forced to wear the chador while men wear Levi's, Diesel and Nike.*

Above: *One Tehran testimony to Iran–US détente.*

as they pored over it and traced the red line with their chubby fingers. Most of them were regarding us with awe and trying to shake our hands when we realised they thought we had started in Beijing and were nearing the end of the epic trip. We laughingly disabused them, tracing the infinitesimally short segment of the line we had traversed, but they scarcely seemed less impressed. Someone fumbled about for a bit of English, and came up with the word 'crazy'. The group took it up, and they all grinned and nodded and swivelled their fingers beside their temples, saying 'Crazy, crazy!' We smiled and nodded back. By the time we left, someone had remembered another bit of their school English. 'Good luck!' they said, waving.

Back on the road again. Here and there, nestled on the sward, were hamlets and villages like something out of the Brothers Grimm — no McDonald's or Starbucks infiltrating village culture here. We had our first night in a stereotypically beautiful Austrian village, houses with steep-pitched, shingle rooves flanking cobblestone streets and high, fir-clad slopes rising beyond them. On our arrival, and before we found a hotel, we located a beer hall and sat out on the terrace raising a stein or two to the first day of the great adventure. And you've got to hand it to them, they know how to make the stuff over there.

The day hadn't been entirely without incident. We were parked in the pouring rain at a tollgate on the Austrian autostrada, each of us searching our pockets and panniers for our wallets, racking our brains to work out what sort of currency to use in Austria and where our cache of that particular currency might be amongst the jumble of our belongings, when Jo rolled in. She went to manoeuvre in beside us, but she hadn't reckoned on the extra width of the panniers. She clipped the booth, and put her bike down. Crunch went her mirror. She and a couple of helpers who came over heaved the bike upright again, but they were a little over-vigorous: over she went the other way, collecting Dave's bike, which went down too. Crunch went his mirror. The sight of a couple of Silk Rider bikes in a heap in the toll plaza seemed to brighten the day for the onlookers, which just goes to show that while the Germans may have invented a word for it, *schadenfreude* is not unknown to the Austrians. We had to scour the motorcycle-parts establishments of Austria for mirrors. We found a replacement for Jo's, but had to jury-rig something for Dave. At least we proved by this impromptu experiment that Jo's panniers could handle the impact of a spill — she and Brendan had opted for the snazzy, streamlined plastic jobs, while the rest of us, doubting the durability of these, had gone for square, utilitarian, aluminium affairs. And in the meantime, Jo was the inaugural and uncontested recipient of the new addition to the Silk Rider honours list: the Plonker of the Day Award.

The next day, we ascended into the Alps — every bit as spectacular and beautiful as New Zealand's Southern Alps — and descended into northern Italy. Again, it was a fairytale landscape, everything just so stereotypically and stylishly Italian. The narrow streets of the small farming villages we passed through were thronged with Mercedes and Audis: the EU sponsors a pretty cushy lifestyle for the farmers of Austria and Italy.

We were in the groove by now. You sleep pretty well the first night, and you find a few aches and pains in strange places after your first long day in the saddle. Your shoulders bug you at first, as you get up to match fitness, and so does your lower back, even with the relatively upright riding position the Dakars force you to adopt. But after a few kilometres under your belt the next day, all those cobwebs are gone. The rider etiquette was settling down, too. Everyone seemed to be checking their mirrors for the reassuring sight of the bike light behind them.

In fact, the only problem we had with our formation arose whenever we came to a town, as they were uniformly fraught with mad Italian drivers. Jo mused that if their sex lives were as passionate as their driving, this was her type of country. They would overtake anywhere, and if there was a sniff of a gap in our line — we were riding in Indian file — they would cut into it. Before long, we'd be scattered through miles of speeding traffic, none of us having any idea where everyone else was or where we were going. On our stops, we talked about riding in close formation a fair bit. Brendan thought it was just something we had to put up with: he reckoned having everyone fend for themselves was less dangerous than riding in close formation. He had a point, but sometimes when we were having an argument about it, there were only four or five of us present. If we were going to stick together, as we must for safety reasons and for the sake of making decent progress, something clearly had to be done. Eventually, even Brendan agreed.

Our countermeasure was something we christened 'the Silk Rider Wedgie', in which we'd form up into a triangle, a lead bike at the apex, two behind to either side with their front axles level with the lead bike's rear sprocket, and three abreast bringing up the rear. This way, we were a compact unit and collectively as wide as a car, and had to be treated more or less like a car by overtaking traffic. It worked a treat. People chafed behind us, leaned on their horns or tried to get amongst us, but we just ignored all that and sailed serenely on.

Once we'd hit the lowlands, we rode the short distance to Venice, a city we had last visited when we took the children there in 1996. The weather was still packing a bit of a sad. We aquaplaned our way into town — not because Venice is built upon a rising sea but because it was raining the way it rains between Westport and Karamea and very few other places we've experienced. We'd been planning to pitch our tents for the night, at a campground handy to the ferry that takes you across to Venice proper, which is on a swampy island in the Gulf of Venice. Gareth, Dave and Jo were keen to start the trip on the footing on which it was to continue, and if we let the flyboys — the stockbrokers and the corporate types — select accommodation after the style to which they had become accustomed in their highly paid, jet-setting jobs, it would be pretty hard on the rest of us. So we were keen to keep it as downmarket as we could at first, reserving the five-star establishments for the times when we really needed a bit of a break. But at Venice, the camping plan went quite literally down the drain. We were drenched on arrival. Instead, we located a motorcamp and hired a couple of caravans. Thankfully, as it was shoulder season, we had that option.

Next day, we woke in the cramped, steamy interior to the smell of soggy socks, gloves and riding gear, but we were in good spirits. Just to help our mood along, the clear skies returned, and after breakfast we set out on foot to comb Venice for Marco sites.

You sometimes hear it said that Italy is just one giant theme-park dedicated to preserving the memory of medieval Europe, and you'd have to regard Venice as its star exhibit. The city was a major port in the ancient world — and, indeed, until quite recently — and the townsfolk were comfortable with water and watercraft. They had to be, because the principal mode of transport was gondolas on the city's network of canals. Sea-borne commerce was the mainstay of the Venetian economy, and the Polo family was among its most prominent merchant families. As the bay silted up and the quality of the port deteriorated, Venice's significance waned, and it got left behind in the race for progress. These days, it is the very antiquity of the place that it relies upon: Venetians have found a place for their ancient city in the modern world, through tourism. Who knows how long it will last, unless modern technology can intervene; as we walked across the Piazza San Marco, we were splashing through seawater as the flood tide rose through the manhole covers. Venice is basically built on a swamp, and for aeons it has been settling slowly into it. Now, of course, the sea is rising, too.

Given the Venetian reverence for the past, there are surprisingly few memorials to the existence of one of the city's most famous past residents. There's a library where Marco's last will and testament is held and the San Lorenzo church, in the yard of which he was buried in 1324, remains. In the area where the Polo homestead was sited, we found ourselves in an area of little courts bearing the name 'Il Milione', and knew we were close: this was Marco's nickname, 'the teller of a million tales'. A man came out of a restaurant when he saw us poking around and told us that the building we were looking at was one of the original buildings associated with the Polo family home, but he was vague about its precise significance. At another site, we found a plaque commemorating Marco himself. Looking out over the city and the bay and reflecting that this was where that great journey began 750-odd years ago was a pretty special feeling.

We were at the start line, and we were all set to go.

Biking the Balkans

We began the trip proper without too much ceremony: just a reading from Marco before setting off. We got onto the autostrada and followed the signs for Trieste, the beginning of unknown territory for all of us. We stayed that night at a little Mediterranean tourist trap called Opicina.

It's only a few kilometres from Opicina to Italy's border with Slovenia, but it might as well be a thousand. The next day, the formalities at the crossing swiftly despatched, we crossed into the first of the Balkan states we were to traverse. It was only a short stretch of road, but the contrast with the conspicuous wealth and sleek style of Italy was stark, and pretty sobering. Suddenly, we weren't sharing the road with the Mercs and the Alfas driven by your average Italian farmer; instead, there were coarsely dressed men and women riding horses or donkeys or rotary hoes, towing trailers loaded with goods or grannies. You do see cars: such internationally acclaimed marques as the Yugo, the Stada and the Zastava. The land is barren and fallow, the houses pathetic, the infrastructure worse — all the result of 50 years of underinvestment under the Tito regime. It was as though we'd ridden into a time warp. And given Slovenia was the least damaged of the former states of Yugoslavia in the grim civil war of the 1990s, it didn't bode too well for the rest of them.

For behaving itself during the collective madness of reprisal and ethnic cleansing during the 1990s and for adapting satisfactorily to the democracy game, Slovenia has been rewarded with full membership of the European Union. The visible emblem of this status is the flash autostrasse the union has constructed across it, surveyed, so far as we could tell, from hilltop to hilltop so as to avoid the seedy villages in which the population lives, and designed to get the rich Europeans more quickly from the north to their playground on the Croatian coast.

That's where we were headed, too: to the island of Korcula, birthplace of Marco Polo, but along the local roads rather than the flash dual carriageway. It was going to be a long way in the pouring rain while we gritted our teeth against jolts delivered through the forks from such poorly maintained bitumen surfaces. It was less accurate to say that the tarseal was badly potholed than to say the potholes were poorly sealed. It was impossible to avoid the huge craters and bone-shaking corrugations; Jo, with her bike's smaller wheels, had a particularly hard time with the corrugations, until Dave advised her to keep her speed up. That way you sort of skim over them. We were pretty tired at the end of that first day's riding in the Balkans. Poor old Phil fared particularly badly with all the jarring, as he suffers from carpal tunnel syndrome in both wrists. A few decent thumps through the forks and he loses all the strength in his grip. It bugged him at night, too, with an unrelenting burning sensation in his fingers.

If Slovenia is a poor cousin of Europe then the next former Yugoslav state we crossed is both poor and sad, and pretty much disowned by the rest of the family of European nations. Thanks to its one major earner, the gem-like coastline which is a mecca for European tourists, Croatia is the richest of the alumni of the disintegrated Yugoslavia through which we passed, but the wealth is merely a veneer. The rest is misery. This, lest we forget, is where in the early 1990s the Eastern Orthodox Serbs and the Catholic Croats slugged it out over the issue of whether Croatia should be allowed to become an independent state. The noes won the first round — something like 10,000 Croats were killed in the early part of the conflict — but history teaches us that no Balkan resident is going to take that kind of treatment quietly. The response was an orgy of tit-for-tat, vicious, vindictive ethnic cleansing.

For this reason, the country of Marco Polo's birth has a very uneasy feel to it. Away from the dramatically beautiful Dalmatian coast, the summer playground for fat Germans and glossy Italians, Croatia is at best an agrarian economy, where the hard lives of its people have been made worse by the cyclical post-Communist era lunges at nationalism. Even for the inhabitants of the area adjoining the gorgeous coastline — covered with hotels that open for just three months a year, and boatyards and marinas patronised by regular visits from the Mediterranean's superyacht fleet — the impression is one of a local population on the outside looking in enviously upon the lifestyles of the rich and famous. They must surely wonder where they would be but for 60-odd years of ethnic purges, village pogroms and the smouldering intolerance of minorities. So visible is the tragedy of Croatia that we dared not discuss with locals the rights and wrongs of the latest turbulence. The wounds are just too recent. We stuck to exchanging tourist trivia with our hosts.

It was quite extraordinary to arrive in some of the towns on the Croatian coast, where we'd see several huge, promising-looking hotels only to find they were completely shut. Asking around, we'd be told that there was no chance of getting hotel accommodation in the off-season, but there was a hostel or a bed-and-breakfast down the road that might have room for six of us. You just don't get that stark contrast between high and low seasons in New Zealand.

The rain dogged us on our six-day traverse of Croatia. But our main mission in this country was, of course, the visit to Korcula, and we were blessed with perfect weather on the day of our pilgrimage. We left five of the bikes at the bed-and-breakfast and caught a ferry out there — we were just about the only people on the passenger boat. Dave and his bike came over on a vehicular ferry, as we wanted to photograph one of the bikes at Marco's birthplace.

The pretty little island (permanent population of 17,000) was practically deserted when we got there. No matter, the locals were only too pleased to open up the Polo house — currently under restoration — where Marco was supposed to have been born. It was quite a big deal for them to have us there; TV and the local newspaper carried pictures and a story. It all helped, we were told, to draw it to the world's attention that Polo was a Croat, contrary to what the Venetians would have you believe.

We had learned through our research — and the locals proudly confirmed it — that Korcula has strong links with New Zealand. Some of our prominent families, such as Auckland's wine-making Nobilo family and Wellington's Belich family, hail from here. You can easily see why the Dalmatian islands are the playground of the Mediterranean superyacht glitterati, and also why there's so much tension between the tourist haves and the local have-nots who must wait on them, hand and foot. The residents of Korcula need the tourist season, but you can tell it's a blessing for them that it's only three months a year.

After a day exploring Korcula and perusing the Marco Polo museum, we cruised on down the coast to Dubrovnik on the border with Bosnia-Herzegovina. This great, ancient, walled city has been completely rebuilt three or four times in its history, the latest reconstruction occasioned by the 1990s civil war, when it was shelled and sustained something like 2000 hits from high-explosive and shrapnel rounds. On our arrival there were five cruise ships in port, and the place was crawling with tourists. We wandered about, happily rubbing shoulders with camera-hung Americans, Germans, Italians and Japanese. It seemed there was a choir or a little orchestra performing on every street corner, each with its small crowd of tourists beaming and applauding. Dubrovnik is clearly the epicentre of Croatian culture.

The following day, 8 km beyond Dubrovnik, we crossed the border with Bosnia-Herzegovina. It was strange, bleak country to be riding in, all tortured beech clinging to craggy rock — only five per cent of the land here is arable — like a moonscape with firewood. Scattered amongst it were shelled-out villages, ten years on still populated with stunned people trying to pick up the pieces left over from the battle for Dubrovnik. Take tourism out of the Croatian equation, and you'll get something like Bosnia. For Bosnia-Herzegovina, without all those euros that Croatia receives from idling tourists, there's no easy way back from the devastation wrought by the latest in its miserable history of nationalist convulsions.

Just how bleak things are was acutely visible in the town of Trebinje, fewer than 30 km up the ridge from Dubrovnik. Instead of crowds of tourists pointing cameras and waving euros, the crowds here consisted of mourners standing, heads bowed, in the huge graveyard. Women in black — widows — rested their empty gaze upon us as we rode through a town where every building was scarred with machine-gun fire, and graffiti pointedly read 'Fuck off NATO'.

We noticed a distinct deterioration in both the roads and the driving as we headed through Bosnia and into Montenegro. Atrocious surfaces wound up through high mountain passes and swooped down into deep, narrow, fertile valleys. There were fewer cars than in Croatia, but it seems road rage is the peacetime outlet for Balkan thuggery: either brakes are an optional extra on older model Yugos and Ladas, or there's a whole generation of Balkan drivers who are unfamiliar with their operation. We lost track of the number of times we were forced over onto the shoulder of the road to avoid certain death under a flying tonne of Eastern European metal. They can't drive for nuts. Bikes, of course, have to look out for everyone's mistakes, because you're the most vulnerable thing on the road.

It goes without saying that Montenegro is poor, and the population barely above the breadline. You'd think, what with the upheavals of the 1990s and the perpetual, grinding poverty, that its population had suffered enough, but more trouble looms. The latest geopolitical configuration has Montenegro part of a temporary-sounding combine named Serbia-Montenegro and, sure enough, there is soon to be a referendum on Montenegro's secession. Polling suggests 95 per cent of Montenegrans will vote for their own independent nation, which Serbia is not going to take to kindly: losing Montenegro would cut off its only access to the Mediterranean and leave it surrounded on every side by unfriendly, if not downright hostile, neighbours. Who knows what the Serbs will do about it, but the turbulent history of this region suggests it won't be decided by everyone joining hands and singing 'Kumbaya'.

The plan after Montenegro was to go into Kosovo, the name of which still rings a dismal bell with most news-watchers from the 1990s. It had been difficult to get much information about how this could be achieved from New Zealand. Most websites were discouraging. We thought our best chance would be to play it by ear when we got to the border, although we knew it would be wise to have a plan B. It turned out our advance information was right, however: we arrived at the border and were met by a bunch of blue-helmeted UN policemen, who explained we could get *into* the UN-controlled state, OK, but getting out would be a problem. Serbia, which surrounds it, doesn't recognise Kosovo, so if we were to enter, the only way we'd be allowed out would be to detour far to the south through Albania and Macedonia. Bugger that. Plan B was to head north through metropolitan Serbia, around Kosovo.

'That way.' The cops indicated a goat track leading up into the rocky, sparsely treed hills.

So it was into Serbia we rode. Here, too, the signs of the recent unrest were fresh. Occasionally we'd stop at a village and ask directions to another village, shown on the map to be only a few kilometres distant. Smiles would fade, people's faces would close, and they'd shake their heads. No one knew about that village, we'd be told. They were the enemy. No one from this village goes there. Tragic stuff, really.

Jo had a close encounter with it in one village. While we were standing around and the usual fuss was being made of us, she noticed one old woman waving to her. She followed, and the woman took her into her run-down little house, the walls scarred with bullet holes. She gave Jo a cup of tea, and they talked, after the fashion of people who don't share a language. She was fascinated by Jo's photo album, particularly the family shots. She pulled out tattered photos of her own, and wept as she showed them to Jo. There was no need for a common language to get the story across. These men were her family — brothers and sons — and they had been killed in the civil war.

Despite its mournful history and the general poverty, there was plenty of human spirit evident. We were greeted virtually everywhere with waves and smiles. Interest was intense wherever we stopped, with crowds gathering at the coffee shops to study the maps on our panniers, and to have a go at sounding out our names as they were written on the bikes and matching them to their riders. Naming our steeds may have seemed like a bit of a wank before we left New Zealand, and we still attract a fair bit of ribbing from Kiwi bikers for having the motorcycle equivalent of geeky conference name-labels, but it proved to be another great tool for breaking down the language barrier abroad.

By now, we were really in the swing of things. Through trial and error, we had pretty much worked out where and how everything should be stowed on our bikes and on our persons, which things we'd need easy access to and which could be safely stowed in the darkest recesses of the panniers. Jo and Brendan were better off than the rest of us in the main, because they had nifty, wide-access lids on their gourmet panniers, whereas we would have to half-dismantle our luggage to get at anything which wasn't right on top. You worked out what you were going to need at night in the hotel, so that you could take only one bag and leave the rest on the bike. And we were watching one another carefully, to see if anyone had figured out a trick or routine that would make our own lives easier.

We stayed in a Serbian town called Leskovac, not altogether one of the world's pleasure spots. The state-owned hotel was straight out of some Peter Sellers comedy: it could have been a Moscow hotel during the Cold War. We were the only guests, and you could see why. The lift was chronically prone to getting stuck between floors, and while there were hot and cold taps in every room — where they hadn't fallen off, as they and doorknobs were wont to do — both delivered cold water only. Tourists just don't come here. And service? It was about what you'd expect from dispirited public servants who draw their low wage no matter how badly the hotel is doing.

Still, Leskovac provided us with another of the highlights of the Balkan leg of our tour. We were sitting in an outdoor café — the only half-clean one in town — and had noticed that apart from a table where there was a nice-looking young man sitting with a couple of girls, we were surrounded by an unusually high concentration of heavy-set, crew-cut blokes in dark glasses and nicely tailored suits. Every now and then, one of these thugs would wander over and exchange a few words with the young man. We wondered what the relationship might be, and had idly surmised that perhaps we had wandered into some kind of Serbian mafia joint.

Suddenly, a line of big black cars drew up outside and disgorged more thugs, who formed a tight knot around a dapper, silver-haired fellow and moved toward the door. Everyone in the café suddenly stood up, except us. We just sat there. The dapper fellow shook hands with a couple of the thugs and with the young man and his two companions. Then he seemed to notice the table where no one was standing up. Our hearts were going a bit. These, we thought, were the renowned 'bullies of the Balkans', and they were about to deliver a taste of Serbian hospitality to these insolent Western interlopers.

Nothing could have been further from the truth. Nudging his way through the wall of biceps, the man advanced, wreathed in smiles and with hand outstretched.

'Hello,' he said. 'Welcome to Serbia. What brings you here?'

'We're from New Zealand. We're on a motorbike tour,' we told him.

Then Brendan stuck out his hand.

'Hello,' he said. 'My name's Brendan. What's yours?'

The man shook hands with Brendan and told him his name. He was, he explained, the deputy prime minister of Serbia — one of the good guys who ousted über-thug Slobodan Milosevic not so long ago.

He sat down at the next table, and the young man and his companions came and joined him, followed by a sizeable contingent of people with notebooks and cameras. An animated conversation in Serbian commenced. After a few minutes, the politician broke off and handed a brochure across to us. On it was the young man's photograph. He was, it turned out, a young Serbian maestro who had lately received critical acclaim following a concert at Carnegie Hall, and the deputy prime minister was here to meet him and congratulate him on his success.

After a while, the dignitary turned his attention to us, and asked us a raft of questions directed at finding out what the hell had induced a bunch of Kiwis to visit backblocks Serbia. The cameras were there and rolling as he listened to our story. He was impressed, he told us, and wished us well — a nice moment of international entente for the Serbian six o'clock news. All the world's a stage!

From Leskovac we headed due east. Our route took us up to the snowline and then suddenly down again. The road was barely more than a country lane with 1.5 m deep snow drifts each side of the road clipping our panniers: it certainly wasn't cambered properly, so we were competing with the spring melt to see who could get down to the valley floor first. This made for slippery riding, but we reached the lowlands again in one piece and spent the night in the beautiful old Bulgarian city of Sofia.

Bulgaria enjoyed a far smoother transition from communism than its miserable Balkan neighbours, and is a full member of the European Union. Our first impression was that the general population enjoys a far higher standard of living than the countries to its immediate west. It has the EU membership card — the fancy, EU-funded autobahn reaching practically right across the country — but no one warned us about one peculiarly Bulgarian road hazard haunting this stretch of superhighway. Gareth, who was leading, passed an intersection with a country road and was confronted by the sight of a young woman standing at the roadside wearing little more than a miniskirt and a professional smile. It was the middle of nowhere. It was all too much for a boy from Putaruru. He experienced his first severe case of 'tank-slap' (the biker's term for the wobbles which accompany losing control through over-vigorous application of the brakes, which causes the bike to fishtail wildly, the handgrips slapping back and forth against the tank) of the trip. He rode on, wondering whether he'd really seen what he thought he'd seen. A few kilometres down the track, and here was a pair of similarly underdressed women. A few more kilometres and here were several more, engaged in negotiations with the drivers of a stationary couple of the huge articulated trucks that ply the Bulgarian superhighway. Jo had her work cut out keeping the boys moving past the long, long line of Highway Women. Capitalism may be in its infancy in Bulgaria, but entrepreneurism is clearly alive and well.

We got a bit lost in one of the towns in Bulgaria, as the signs were all in Cyrillic script. Gareth solved the problem by coaxing one of the local beauties to ride pillion and show us the way. As he turned the corner, a huge grin across his face, he became aware of a shriek from the back of his bike. It was his passenger, convinced Gareth was taking her to her death under an articulated truck: he'd instinctively gone to the left-hand side of the carriageway, and was confronted by a wall of traffic. Luckily, the Dakars are built for use on- and off-road, so he bumped up and over the median strip and onto the correct side of the road. His shaken passenger showed us the way and waved us goodbye without looking that sorry to see us go.

The ravages of communism were clearly to be seen throughout Bulgaria. The towns were typical of those from which the Soviet tide has rolled back: impoverished and characterised by ablution-block architecture, with traces here and there of a kind of regeneration. If the hotels are anything to go by, regeneration has a way to go, though. Most of them were half built, and they charged 'special', exorbitant prices for tourists. That's almost certainly why we were the only occupants.

From Jo's point of view, the best feature of the towns — or at least, two of the ones we passed through — were the trolleybuses. Bus-nut Jo, a card-carrying member of the Omnibus Society, was as great a danger to herself and others as she rode past ogling the trolleybuses as any of the boys were around the Highway Women. She seriously got off on the varying types of overhead and how well hung it was.

The hill country in the west toward the border with Greece was spectacular, but we learned there are hydroelectricity schemes afoot that may change all that. As usual, we found travelling in the

Bulgarian countryside far more congenial than the towns. At one village where we stopped, we were approached in the town square by a man anxious to get us along to the nearby school where he taught. Bryan and Gareth weren't keen: Gareth was struggling with a bad cold at this point, and nothing was going to get between him and a badly needed cup of coffee. Jo and the others went along, though. Their arrival caused quite a stir. The girls poured into the playground and surrounded the bikes while the Silk Riders were plied with coffee in the staff room. Jo availed herself of the headmistress' internet connection to show her the Silk Rider website and, as a quid pro quo, checked a few emails. Then the four of them split up and visited the classrooms. The kids goggled at them in their astronaut gear. They explained to the students as best they could who they were, where they were from and where they were going. The blow-up globe and photo albums helped get the message across.

Afterward, by which time Gareth and Bryan had rejoined, we showed the kids the bikes, and Dave managed, after protracted negotiations, to persuade the headmistress to sit on his bike for a photo. She did so, pretty diffidently. Dave then suggested he take her for a spin for a block or so, so that she could show us the way out of town. Well, that was just too far outside her comfort zone. She couldn't possibly do that. We left her with a handful of New Zealand coins, a few bits of paua shell and a couple of the printed cards we were carrying.

She waved wistfully after us, while we reflected what a privilege it is to drop into people's lives the way we had just done, hang out with them for a while, then at the push of a button sweep on again, ready for the next adventure. The joy of motorcycle touring.

Talking Turkey

Bryan was an early riser. He liked to get up before the rest of us and get on with the routine daily maintenance of the bikes — making sure the chains were oiled, the tyre pressures and the fluid levels were right, that kind of thing. For the first half of the trip, Phil was his room-mate, and tended to get up at the same time and give him a hand. Early rising took its toll, however: come evening, and the end of a long day's ride, those two took themselves off to bed pretty early.

Brendan and Dave, on the other hand, were night owls. They liked to get down into the town, schmoozing around girls or whatever it was they did, until the wee hours. Jo, who after Dave was the most gregarious in the group, would sometimes go with them, or wander about by herself. The best way to see a new place, she reckons, is on your own. People are more likely to approach you and talk to you if you're by yourself than if you've got company.

Gareth, however, after a beer or two and dinner at the end of the day, tended to prefer to write or read and, regardless of whether it was exactly what he felt like doing, he spent a lot of his time in the evenings uploading photos to the Silk Riders website or answering emails. Or at least, this was his excuse at those times when, misanthrope that he is, he just didn't feel like socialising.

We were a compatible group, about as good as you're likely to get and certainly the best we'd been involved with in our bike-touring career, but harmony so often depends on everyone getting their little bit of time alone.

The border of a country is always a good place to form first impressions, and our first impressions of Turkey were not good. We had no fewer than five passport and carnet checks to endure, for which we each had four stamps in our passports to show at the end of a long, tedious hour.

The long delay on top of an arduous ride — we'd ridden right across Bulgaria, covering the better part of 300 km since leaving Sofia that morning — obviously got to Dave. He was so confused by matters that he went to the money exchange and sort of melted down, asking them to change his stock of euros back into Bulgarian stotinki. He just about needed a wheelbarrow to carry off the pile of notes he received. Too late, he realised he should have been changing his remaining stotinkis for euros. There was no contest for Plonker of the Day award that day!

Once across the border, we found ourselves cruising past a 10 km queue of trucks pointing in the opposite direction, all bumper to bumper with their drivers smoking and drinking tea next to them, waiting to get their rigs and their payload out of Turkey. Then, the trucks left behind, we were gunning our bikes along the 25 km stretch of highway to Edirne without another soul upon it. There was, we decided, something screwy about this country. Turkey wants into the European Union: from our experience, if it's subjected to the rigours of competition and efficiency expected of member states, it will be slaughtered.

The following day, we took a day off the Silk Road traverse and headed for Gallipoli. It was a significant time to be there: it was ninety years since the New Zealand Expeditionary Force landed there in 1915, but we had deliberately timed our pilgrimage a couple of days after Anzac Day so we could avoid the mayhem that the annual commemoration ceremony has become, and give the Turkish authorities time to clean up the rubbish the hordes leave behind.

The intention was to pitch our tents near the beach at Anzac Cove and, given fine weather, swim in the Aegean Sea there and look up at the infamous cliffs that stood between the Anzacs and a realistic chance of getting across the Gallipoli Peninsula. But the rain as we rode into Gelibolu township was torrential so we moved to plan B — staying put and joining an organised tour of the Gallipoli National Park with a Turkish guide. This, as it turned out, was a good way to go: it was both interesting and informative, and very moving.

It took about an hour in a steamy, cramped van to get to Anzac Cove. Our first sight of the scene of the action was from a distance, and you could immediately see just what a tragedy the whole affair was. Instead of being landed a kilometre away, where the flatter terrain offered a far more realistic chance of gaining the interior of the peninsula, they were set ashore at the foot of steep cliffs — the closest local comparison is the sheer limestone pinnacles on the Wairarapa's south coast — which they were expected to scale under withering fire from the Turks entrenched on the high ground.

For all the slaughter that followed, that part of the coastline was only lightly defended at the time, as the Turks had no idea anyone would be mad or foolish enough to land there. Amazingly, on that first day of the campaign, April 25, 1915, six Kiwis actually got up onto Chunuk Bair, the highest point on the peninsula. There they saw the Dardanelles — the campaign's strategic objective — in the distance and, nearer at hand, 15,000 Turks hurrying their way. They decided discretion was the better part of valour, and headed back down for 'reinforcements'. It was four months before New Zealanders again stood on Chunuk Bair, the climax of the bloody campaign.

The Anzacs made inroads on the outnumbered Turkish forces from their beachhead, our guide explained. But the retreating Turks were met by their commander, Mustafa Kemal, who told his troops that he wasn't ordering them to attack, he was ordering them to die. While they died, he promised, reinforcements would arrive to win the day. Then, our guide told us with tears in his eyes, he issued the most inspirational part of his order: 'Follow me.' This was in stark contrast to the orders issued to the Anzacs by their absentee High Command: 'No retreat, dig and get buried.'

Kemal survived that assault, and all the others, and went on (as Ataturk, 'the father of Turkey') to lead Turkey after the war in its transition from the rule of the sultans of the Ottoman Empire days.

We defy any New Zealander to make this trip and remain unmoved. Standing on the ground at Gallipoli you realise what a crime was committed there, emotionally at least. Three thousand young New Zealanders died in that campaign, sacrificed by the callous command whose agenda was completely out of New Zealand control. And they were so young: we made a point of visiting every grave we could find that contained a New Zealander and reading the inscriptions; we were shocked to find that while most were in their very early 20s and some were as old as 30, there were quite a few who were as young as 15 or 16. Gallipoli is really a monument to the irrationality of war, a reminder of how the value of these young people's lives was virtually zero to those who knew the odds and had the power to order a withdrawal. What a colossal waste. Never again.

From Gallipoli, we headed in torrential rain for Istanbul. On the way, we stopped in a muddy little village for coffee. While we were settling down in the coffee house, Jo noticed a girl waving from an upstairs window and waved back. When the boys looked up, a curtain fell across. Presently, a gate in the corrugated-iron fence at street level opened, and a young girl shyly emerged. She looked at Jo, but when she saw the blokes looking at her, she blushed and giggled as though she'd been caught skinny-dipping and ducked back behind the gate, which closed with a bang. Jo went and knocked and let herself in.

Inside, there were dozens of women packed into the little yard, who gave her a rapturous welcome. More women, from girls to grannies, arrived all the time. They pressed around her, asking questions in their own language, in whatever scraps of English they could find and in the more universal sign language. They studied the route map and exclaimed delightedly over the photograph album. 'Kiwi!' they said, pointing to Jo. 'Kiwi!' If they'd had their way, Jo would have eaten with them and stayed all day, but the rest of us were gearing up ready to take off. She said her farewells, and reluctantly re-entered the world of men through the iron gate.

From here, we followed a narrow, winding road which had been converted by weeks of rain to a kind of sluggishly flowing river of mud. We slithered and slid our way along, feeling pretty vulnerable for the most part. We were already tired by the time we reached the outskirts of Istanbul, and prepared to take on what had been rumoured to be some of the worst traffic in the world. This, of course, entailed forming the Silk Rider Wedgie again and toughing it out. We were beginning to learn that it was to our advantage to put Jo in front, because she was the one who caused the most pandemonium as Middle Eastern drivers just stopped and stared at her, no matter what the prevailing road or traffic conditions, or started gesticulating wildly to get the attention of the first woman they'd ever seen on a motorbike.

We made staccato progress into the city. The bikes, which are water cooled and depend on a decent airflow through the radiator to stay within operating range, started to overheat, and if you weren't careful about keeping your revs up at idle, you'd stall. This happened a few times, and each time it was a bit of a struggle to get started again. None of this, of course, did anything to alleviate the stress of battling with the traffic in the Turkish capital.

When you're on a bike, there's got to be something pretty special about a city before you'd bother braving the particular hazards of traffic congestion and ill-tempered drivers. Istanbul, we all agreed, just didn't cut it. There were some fantastic mosques, and it's one of the great cities from a historical and geographical perspective, but it just doesn't compare to Paris, or Prague, or any one of those other major European cities. It was dirty, untidy and unkempt and the bloody awful weather which prevailed throughout our time there didn't help. None of us was that sorry to leave it, awakened as we were at half-past four in the morning by the amplified call of the muezzin from the nearest minaret, his cry swiftly taken up by the massed voices of the dogs of Istanbul. Turkey is a big country — nearly 70 million people, 99 per cent Muslims — and there's a lot of dogs.

As we travelled east through Turkey, Gareth was becoming concerned about the performance of his bike. It had not escaped his attention — nor, to his discomfort, had it escaped everyone else's, for we gave him arseholes — that he was going through petrol at a far higher rate than anyone else. There must be a fuel mixture problem, he thought, or something of that nature going on. He and Bryan discussed it. Bryan suggested they eliminate the possible causes one by one, starting with the easiest: the rider. They swapped bikes. When they compared consumption at the next fuel stop, it was clear that the fuel economy of Bryan's bike had collapsed underneath Gareth, whereas his bike was doing as well as Bryan's did under Bryan. The cause of the excessive fuel consumption was clear: Gareth's penchant for engine-braking and for impetuously wrenching the throttle open out of corners.

We began to enjoy ourselves a lot more as we truly settled into the pattern of the days on the Silk Road. We'd start off at eight in the morning after breakfast and a reading. (It's funny how carefully the locals trod around us in places like Turkey and Iran while Gareth read from Marco's book: they clearly thought this was some kind of religious observance.) We'd ride for a couple of hours before finding a suitable village in which to stop for coffee and a breather. The best places to go tended to be the 'smoking dens', which are the meeting-places of the local population — or at least the male half. This is where the men would gather with their thick, sweet coffee and their thick, sweet tobacco smoke and yak, mostly about politics. This being the case, as you can well imagine, the snarl of the Silk Rider bikes arriving in town tended to brighten the day for the locals. We'd haul in and instantly be surrounded by crowds of shouting, waving people. We'd clown about while they tried out their English on us. It wasn't that hard to make ourselves understood, despite having almost no words in common. We weren't that surprised people had heard of the New Zealand connection with Gallipoli, but it came as a slight shock that when we mentioned our native land, people were just as likely to break into a smile and say: 'Frodo! Sam! Lord of the Rings!' as 'Kiwi!' To our great gratification, people would pick out the words 'Marco Polo' on the pannier maps, and immediately respond to the adventurer's name. It was a long time since he'd passed this way, but he hadn't been forgotten.

Wherever we went, we'd be virtually dragged into the nearest smoking den, and as many people as possible would pack in after us. In some of the villages, the locals even posted their own guards over our gear while we were inside. Yarns were swapped, lies were told, bonhomie was all about. We had to fight to be allowed to pay for our coffee.

Curiously, although the smoking dens are strictly off limits for Turkish women, Jo was not only welcomed, but frequently made the centre of attention. For Turkish men, usually strictly segregated from women, the chance to talk to Jo was not to be missed. As a 'guest', the only real concession she seemed to have to make to Islam was to cover her head, which she did with a scarf; so long as her head was covered, no one had a problem at all, at least in the comparatively liberal western part of the country. And more than that, while she could move freely in the men's world, her gender also gave her an entrée into a world that was forbidden to the boys. Here and there in the villages where we stopped, while the lads were gassing with the locals, Jo would be off wandering. A hand would emerge from a window and beckon to her urgently. She'd be admitted to a house and, within minutes, women would be packing into the yard, covered from head to foot in the street but gratefully casting back their coverings once inside.

These little villages are where it's at on a bike trip. We'd stop in two or three per day's ride, and get an enthusiastic welcome. No traffic, people with time to spend with you: you can be a mere 30 km from a major population centre and modern city such as Istanbul and you'll feel as though you're a million miles — and at least a century — away. The pace of life, the way things are done make it seem as though nothing has changed from ancient times. It has to be said that they can afford this particular luxury because the European Union is anxious to shore up its neighbours, including the former allies of the Soviet bloc as it seeks to assemble a bloc of its own sufficient to rival the United States as the bastion of Western democracy. It expresses this wish by subsidising the traditional lifestyles of 'European' villagers.

Our route next took us up to northern Turkey, a long, long day to Amasra on the shores of the Black Sea, where the locals were very surprised to see us. No foreigners but Russians go there at this time of year, they told us, and it was easy to see why. It was bitterly cold, and the weather was atrocious. The trade-off to avoid being fried in the great deserts of the East was always going to be enduring the cold at this end of the journey, but as we shivered our way along the Black Sea coast, our fingers numbed to the bone despite winter gloves and electric handwarmers, the idea of being too hot seemed laughable. We were not impressed by Amasra, nor by Samsun or Tirebolu, the other 'resort' towns up here. They were shabby places, where every second house was unfinished and the hotels were miserable, broken-down affairs. Still, we had no complaints about the people. After a session at an internet café one day, as Gareth was walking along the footpath, a group of youngsters ran up and handed him some coins. The proprietor of the café had overcharged him, they gave him to understand, and the locals had stood over the malefactor until he handed over his ill-gotten gains.

At another spot, we were drinking coffee in one of the smoking dens, Jo included. There was another den across the road, two storeys high and full of Turkish men, drinking coffee and smoking. Phil nudged Jo and pointed across to it.

'Bet you can't get in there,' he said.

Gareth turned around a few minutes later and there, across the road, was Jo, surrounded by men on the balcony of the smoking den. The direct approach had worked for her again. She had strode in, greeted everyone on the ground floor, climbed the stairs and lined up the man who looked most senior among the astounded crowd of Turks.

'Hello,' she called, holding out her map. 'I'm from New Zealand.'

After a moment's confusion, a cup was found for her and filled with tea.

'How the hell did she get up there?' Gareth wanted to know.

'I dared her to,' said Phil. 'I reckon she's crossing thresholds that women have never crossed before.'

Similarly, in the same village, Jo was out walking by herself and had attracted a group of schoolboys, all in their late teens. Her presence, unaccompanied and with her head uncovered, captivated them. They pressed around her, eager to ask questions and to look at the photographs in her album. They were, predictably, particularly taken with the photographs of our daughters.

'Do you need a husband for your daughter?' they would ask, and the whole group, Jo included, would roar with laughter. It was unforgettable.

Going about by herself was potentially a risky business, but Jo trusted her gut instinct. Occasionally she would get the sense that all was not well. Mostly, though, she had no problems, and it is a testament to how much all peoples have in common that her instincts never let her down on this trip.

But Turkey is a big country, and spans some ancient ethnic divides. As we travelled eastwards toward Iran, close to the borders with Georgia and Armenia, the people became far less European and visibly more Central Asian. Since Serbia, we had been seeing more and more minarets. By the time we reached eastern Turkey, no village, no matter how poor, was without one. The housing changed from the Western style, and most villages were crowded with mud-roofed adobe shanties. In his regular radio interview with Paul Holmes by sat-phone, Gareth described it as 'the Papua New Guinea of Central Asia', and the description was pretty apt. The east is substantially poorer than the rest of Turkey — it has missed out on the levels of investment the parts closer to Europe enjoy — and social attitudes become correspondingly more conservative the farther east you go. The women are really under the thumb in these parts, and became even less willing to engage — although they were not so oppressed that Jo couldn't coax a gesture or so of solidarity from the fully veiled 'lesser species'. Women became less and less visible altogether. The internet cafés, or some of them, at least, started featuring signs saying 'Girls Welcome', although even in these we didn't see many brave enough to exercise this limited right to be in a public place. We reached a tacit understanding amongst ourselves that there was to be no more joking about Jo's marital status vis-à-vis the five of us. The best thing to do for whoever was with her, apart from Gareth, was to say they were her brother. People backed off in a hurry when the boys introduced themselves thus in the Muslim countries, where traditionally brothers look after their sisters.

In one village, as the usual crowd milled around, a child urgently tugged on Gareth's sleeve. He gesticulated at the seat where Gareth had put his sunglasses a moment before turning his back, and pointed at a kid pushing his way through the onlookers. The glasses were missing. Gareth set off in pursuit. The kid, who was free of the crowd by now, sneaked a look back and saw him coming. He set the glasses down carefully on the footpath and took to his heels. Gareth retrieved his glasses. No fuss, no foul.

We struck a glitch of sorts in Erzurum, eastern Turkey. We had checked into a dodgy-looking hotel, gone out in search of the evening meal — what else but a doner kebab? — and on our return crowded into the tiny hotel lift. The usual jokes about sucking in your stomach, eating fewer kebabs and skipping the baklava in future and for god's sake nobody fart went around. The doors closed, then promptly flew open again.

We clearly had to jettison some of the payload, and by unanimous vote Bryan and Dave, the heftiest of us all, jumped out. This time, the doors closed and the lift lurched into motion — but not for long. It stuck fast, just a little way into its upward journey. As the temperature in the elevator car rose rapidly, Jo, Gareth, Phil and Brendan could hear Bryan and Dave wetting themselves laughing and the hotel staff holding an animated conversation.

The staff didn't seem to have much of a clue what to do, but they allowed Bryan and Dave to have a go at resetting the lift motors. No luck. Bryan, Dave and the staff began to formulate a rescue strategy while those of us trapped within got as comfortable as we could: four fully grown bikers to a 1 sq m space. Phil began to get a bit edgy, as claustrophobia set in, and Gareth was convinced the oxygen was running out.

Between those on the outside and those on the inside, we managed to get the doors open and found there was a gap of about 40 cm between the bottom of the jammed lift and the top of the doorway to the floor below.

'Come on,' Bryan and Dave coaxed. 'You can all get out there!'

Phil was all for having a go at getting out right away, but Dave made him wait while he fetched a large concrete block to wedge in the gap, just in case the lift should start moving upward when some hapless Silkie was halfway out. Frighteningly, Jo produced a large pot of Vaseline and ordered Phil to strip.

'I'll Vaseline you from head to toe and you'll pop through that gap like a pea out of a pod,' she said, with a malicious gleam in her eye.

With that thought to motivate him, and with a little shoving from inside the lift and pulling from without, a fully clothed Phil extruded himself through the gap. The lift actually lurched upward a few centimetres as soon as he was clear, an indication of how wise Dave's concrete-block precaution was. The rather more svelte Brendan, Jo and Gareth then made good their escape. There were two causes for celebration: we were out of the lift not too much the worse for wear (although, as we subsequently discovered, Phil suffered heavy bruising to his ribs), and the lid had stayed on the dreaded Vaseline.

By the following morning, the lift had been fixed. We were careful not to overload it and, just in case, Phil took the stairs. The management of the hotel seemed pretty pleased to see the back of us. Our troubles weren't over, though. There had been a heavy summer dump of snow which had closed the 2300 m pass beyond Erzurum, forcing us to sit tight, about 150 km short of where we needed to be to make all our connections for the border crossing into Iran. Dave was all for going, Phil was all for staying. The rest of us were in the middle. Erzurum is pretty high, but we needed to go even higher to get over to Agri. Bryan impressively deployed the knowledge of atmospherics he had gathered in his career in commercial aviation, calculating how much worse the snow would be that many metres higher. Dave insisted it would be all right. Much to his annoyance, we vetoed going any further until it cleared. We sat around chafing for a few hours, the snow intensifying briefly. Then, miraculously, it stopped. We gave it half an hour or so, then set off. The snow was thick on the ground, and it was bitingly cold riding, but it was beautiful, absolute picture-postcard stuff. It was nowhere near as bad as our flyboy, Bryan, had predicted, which we pointed out at our first stop.

'Glad we're not flying with you!' we told him.

We got over the high, slippery pass and descended to Agri in the region of Turkey that borders Iran. This is Kurd territory, and the attitudes of the population seemed markedly more hardline. It's possible to consider the dress code enforced upon women in Islam as paradoxically quite liberating — it offers privacy from the otherwise oppressive stares of the men when you're in public — but it is nevertheless an emblem of some pretty sick attitudes to women, and it was probably only a matter of time before we had a more tangible demonstration of these.

We had gone into Agri, a sizeable village, where we were intending to stay the night. It was a pretty dismal sort of place, with dirt streets and ramshackle buildings, despite its size. We had a look at a hotel which we found far from inviting. Jo asked where she could find a toilet and was directed down a long, dark alley with no lighting whatsoever but reeking of excrement. Needless to say, her impressions of the place were far from favourable.

Before we made our minds up as to whether to stay or to go on, we thought we'd have a coffee and think about it. We parked in the dirt road in front of a building we were led to believe was a coffee house, and the usual crowd materialised and stood, staring at us and our bikes. It turned out the store wasn't a coffee shop, and nor was there anywhere in the immediate vicinity where we could buy coffee or food. A man from an internet café kindly offered to make us a cup of coffee and, while he was doing this, Gareth got out his laminated map and was showing it to some of the locals to get the conversation going.

The others, meanwhile, didn't feel quite right about things. Bryan, in particular, was nervous. He sidled over to Gareth.

'I don't like the smell of this place,' he said. 'Look at that prick over there. He's going to pinch something if we don't watch out. I've already stopped one of them. Let's get out of here as quick as we can.'

Even Brendan, who usually managed to stay relaxed in the crowd scenes, was nodding.

Gareth dismissed their concerns, although more and more people were pushing into the crowd, and there was a rising note of urgency in the babble of voices.

'Dunno about you guys, but I'm out of here,' Bryan said. He mounted his bike, fired her up and steered through the gap which the crowd opened for him. Phil followed and, after a bit, so did Dave.

Gareth was still talking to an attentive group of locals when he heard a crash and some kind of commotion behind him. He turned to see Jo and her bike on the ground. She's fallen off, he thought.

But there was something about the scene that wasn't quite right. Several white-bearded men were moving forward to help her, flapping their hands at a group of surly looking youths, who slowly backed off. Gareth and Brendan rushed to help her get her bike upright again.

'They pushed me off,' she said, apparently unhurt but clearly a little shaken.

They helped her get her bike started.

'Go!' Gareth told her. 'Just go!'

Jo hauled out, with Gareth and Brendan taking up positions behind her to cover her rear. It was a few miles out of town when the long day and the unsavoury episode caught up with her, and Jo shed a few tears inside her helmet. Marco Polo described the people of this area as 'an evil generation'. You would have been hard pressed to get Jo to disagree.

You would hope that the European Union will continue to withhold the benefits of membership so long as half of the Turkish population is denied its basic human rights. Even so, we could see signs that gave us hope: even the most abject of mud-walled hovels has a satellite dish on its roof, which means that images from the western, liberalised part of Turkey are beaming into the Stone Age east. Change must surely follow.

Irate in Iran

We'd all lost a bit of weight by now: you get pretty fit riding bikes on rough roads, and all of us were experiencing what you might call, for delicacy's sake, digestive problems. Dave's downsizing was perhaps the most dramatic: as he was going down the stairs of the hotel one morning with his hands full of gear, we noticed he had to keep stopping, putting his gear down and hitching up his pants. We started calling him 'the Plumber', in honour of the coy plumber's crack he had begun to show. There was another spin-off, too, and quite a fortuitous one at that. Bryan had miraculously stopped snoring. They say there's a link between any extra weight you're carrying and your tendency to snore. Well, we're believers. As soon as he'd dropped a couple of pounds, we never heard another snort out of one of the most celebrated snorers in New Zealand motorcycle touring.

By this stage of the trip, one little routine had been quietly dropped. We no longer referred to the Plonker of the Day Award, and it was a while since it had been given out. As stress levels rise, you tend to avoid anything that might aggravate them. At the end of a hard day's ride, the last thing you need is everyone labelling you a plonker, particularly if it's become something of a habit. Morale becomes too important.

We had nearly as much trouble getting out of Turkey as we had getting in. The delays were interminable: it can take a truck four days to get across the border, we were told. We were lucky, detained only a few hours. The sticking point, of course, was how much money we needed to give the officials to let us through. The bloke who met us to help us through the formalities was clearly just working us, so we were hanging tough on the figure we were prepared to hand over. Perhaps they just picked on the one making the most noise, but they siphoned Gareth off into a little wire-netting compound in which several other people were waiting their turn to be interviewed in one or other of the sheds. Lots of animated conversation was going on, and every now and then someone would be pushed around by the 'officials'. This helped Gareth focus, while the other Silk Riders sat by their bikes a few metres away enjoying the breakfast they'd looted from the hotel and waving at Gareth in his cage. He noticed that pretty much everyone was paying, so when his turn came, he handed over the equivalent of NZ$12 that they were demanding, without demur — or at least without much.

Finally, with all the right stamps on all the right bits of paper, we were waved through into Iran.

We met Mansuer, Silk Road Adventures' local representative, at Bazargan at ten the following morning. He was to accompany us as a guide through half of our transit of the country — a slightly irritating necessity, but a necessity nonetheless, the price you pay for an 'invitation' to this country. It was a bloody rort, of course, but we had negotiated to be rid of him by the time we got through Tehran. At least we'd be free for the second half of Iran. He was a short, wiry, hyperactive little fellow in a tight T-shirt and tight Levi's that Jo was convinced had a pair of socks stuffed down the front. He strutted about consulting a clipboard and issuing orders, which we pointedly ignored. But we were stuck with him, so with Mansuer in his battered little Suzuki in our wake, we hit the road for Tabriz, 260 km away.

Riding was pretty hairy. You'd be cruising along at 100 km/h when all of a sudden there'd be a Hillman Hunter alongside you, 10 cm from your foot-peg, with an Iranian gazing at you from his rolled-down window, his bristling moustache stretched by a grin. 'Welcome to Iran,' he'd say, or 'Do you need help?' You got the impression that if you showed any inclination, he'd shake your hand through the window, other road users go hang. And once we'd come to terms with the rest of the population, there was always Mansuer to contend with. He'd come belting up at around 150 km/h and cut in front of us to reassure us he was still in contact. After a couple of episodes of this, Dave cornered him at one of our stops, literally picked him up by the scruff of the neck and told him in no uncertain terms that the next time he did that would be the last. When Dave issues threats, people tend to listen.

Perhaps the most distinctive feature of Iran from the saddle was the phenomenon we'd come to refer to as 'road lice', after numerous encounters with it in the countries we'd already traversed. In Iran, it reached plague proportions. As we neared a centre of population, word of our approach would somehow precede us, and a swarm of bareheaded, T-shirt-wearing Iranians on bikes and scooters would materialise in a cloud of blue two-stroke oil-smoke to escort us into town. We'd needed to obtain special permission to take our 650 cc bikes into Iran, as their laws limit engine capacity to 125 cc in town, 200 cc in the country. Their lack of power notwithstanding, small bikes are incredibly popular, particularly among young Iranian men who, with nothing much else to do, petrol a mere 16 cents per litre and a range on a full tank of nearly 1000 km, spend much of their time cruising the highways and byways. They're not dissimilar, we supposed, to our own boy racers. Certainly they share the impulse to show off. Dozens of these bloody things would surround us, mostly ridden two- or even three-up — biker talk for carrying one or two pillion passengers — weaving in and out of us and other traffic, performing hair-raising overtaking manoeuvres and other miscellaneous stunts. Towards the end of our traverse through Tehran, one of them — two-up, of course — was to execute a 200 m wheel-stand, managing to weave through us and a line of cars at the same time, a feat which took our breath away. The difference between this bunch and the rest of the population of the countries we went through was that there was a slight edge to their attention, such as you get with youth gangs of every description in all parts of the world. At times it was possible to enjoy their vibrancy, their energy. But they were out to provoke a reaction, and Phil and Bryan, the older two in our group, got steamed up pretty quickly when they appeared, whether it was weaving amongst us on the road, or tooting the horns or turning the keys on our bikes when we were stopped in the towns. Even the unflappable Dave shouted at one or two of them on occasion.

Jo, of course, tended to attract the most attention. Most of these kids had never seen a woman aboard a motorbike, and when they noticed her they would go ballistic, surrounding her and communicating, by word and gesture, all kinds of comments and propositions. It was all pretty harmless, but bound to engage the protective instincts of your male Kiwi biker. Our response, of course, was the Silk Rider Wedgie, which defied the best attempts of the road lice to break it up. We'd form up as soon as we saw the swarm approaching and just barrel through them, outstripping most of them with our superior acceleration and, let's not deny it, nudging a few of them aside with our hard panniers. We left a few young Iranian fellows with gravel rash to remember us by.

In eastern Turkey, and especially Iran, we had plenty of opportunity to admire asses. Donkeys, of course, are the only kind of ass on display in Islamic regions, and you see them everywhere. Marco Polo, journeying through this part of the world, remarked on their surefootedness and their capacity for carrying prodigious loads. Nothing much has changed in this regard. And the other timeless feature of the Iranian landscape were the flocks of sheep and goats grazing the common land along the roadsides. Each flock, usually comprising up to a hundred assorted sheep and goats, is tended by a shepherd, usually a young boy, with an ass to carry his food and shelter and only a dog for company. The lot of these young shepherds has hardly changed, so far as we could tell, from Biblical times and beyond, except that he has had to add speeding Hillman Hunters to his reckoning of the dangers menacing his flock. There are no fences on Iranian roads, so he must ensure that not only do his charges have feed and water but they are also kept clear of the carriageway. It's quite a sight when you're doing 100 km/h along a modern freeway crammed with cars, trucks and road lice to see a hundred-odd sheep and goats going on their unhurried way on the roadside, with the shepherd, his dog and his donkey following. Just one of the contrasts of Iran. We waved to the shepherds as we passed, and they never failed to grin and wave back.

Before our visit none of us, least of all Gareth, was disposed to like Iran. The image we had of it, derived from the Western media of course, is of a fundamentalist religious dictatorship, populated by chanting, fist-waving, flag-burning Islamic crowds who prostrate themselves to Mecca on the hour every hour. Not a bit of it. Their regime sucks, it's true, but the people are lovely and, in contrast with eastern Turkey, there's a safe, normal feel to things. There are no visible signs of the grinding poverty afflicting most of Eastern Europe — there's no begging, the children are well dressed, happy and look cared for. The mosques didn't seem to be doing as much business as they do in, say,

Pakistan, and there wasn't much evidence of Islamic fundamentalism at street level. There's no harassment in the market and, their horrendous driving notwithstanding, the Iranians are wonderful. We caused chaos wherever we went, of course, and not just because of our (to their eyes) huge bikes. The locals seemed desperate to get an impression of themselves from us. The most common question was 'What do you think of Iran?', followed closely by 'What do you think of Iranian people?', both asked with a mixture of anticipatory pride and mild anxiety.

Their treatment of women is unacceptable to all who value human rights. The men are thoroughly Westernised, and swagger about in tight Levi's and T-shirts, while the women are dressed as though it's the Dark Ages. A kind of apartheid prevails on the buses, where women must sit at the back or stand, even if there are empty seats in the front. It recalls South Africa before Mandela, or Alabama before Martin Luther King. The chador is compulsory, and the mufti 'fashion police' are everywhere, descending on indecently dressed women — those whose tent-like garments show the shape of their hips, or whose hair is visible beneath their head-coverings — to tell them to cover up. The only place, so far as we could tell, where the fanaticism of the mullahs has taken root in the general population is among a class of young, ill-educated and idle men who, doubtless seeing the mysogyny of the regime is to their advantage, take any opportunity to remind women of it. The women hate the prevailing state of affairs, but they are powerless to change it and the men are too scared to help them.

In one restaurant where we had a meal, Brendan heard feminine laughter coming from upstairs. Understandably tired of staring at male faces, he decided he'd investigate, so he armed himself with a handful of picture cards and climbed the stairs. The group of women sitting at their meal fell silent, some of them fumbling to cover their faces, then burst out laughing. Our lady-killing Brendan went around the room, handing out cards, shaking hands and exchanging greetings, while the women laughed and shook their heads, doubtless wondering who this dork was who didn't know there was a law against this kind of carry-on. For, sure enough, there is a law against men being friendly with women in Iran. The poor old restaurateur came sprinting up the stairs flapping his hands at Brendan, explaining in excited pidgin that he must get the hell out of that room.

Similarly, at a place where we were staying, a couple of young girls asked Brendan and Dave if they would like to go with them for a walk in the park and a coffee. They readily agreed, but then the girls lost their nerve, and asked Jo to go along as a chaperone. It would just be asking for too much trouble to be seen, scandalously, in the company of strange men. As it was, Gareth reminded the lads that the girls were young enough to be their grandchildren.

At another village, we were sitting in a coffee house writing little stories in English for the gaggle of kids who were hanging about, and who wanted something they could take to school to read out. One of them asked Jo if she would like to join his mother next door for a cup of tea. She followed, and was met at the door to the yard by the women of the household, who showed her into the garden and gave her a piece of soap to wash herself at the basin there. This, of course, is all part of their hospitality. While she was standing there, she heard a male voice. One of the girls opened a door and, through it, Jo could see a pot-bellied man leaning back on a pile of cushions. Their eyes met. Jo walked straight into the room and extended her hand.

'Hello,' she said 'I'm Jo. I'm from New Zealand.'

The man shook her hand weakly, his face a picture of consternation. Then, as though he didn't know what else to do, he moved over and patted the cushions next to him. Jo sat down. The women goggled from the doorway, apparently afraid to cross the threshold, and laughing as though she had made the greatest and most grievous of all foolish mistakes. This was, she got the distinct impression, a male domain. She was a trespasser here.

The man eventually recovered. As in many of the countries through which we travelled, the men were prepared to cut this poor, ignorant Western woman some slack.

Not everywhere, though. We were refused entry to one Iranian hotel because they wouldn't admit a woman of such depravity that she would go about with five men to whom she was not related.

And all of us found the peremptory manner of the class of un-uniformed law-enforcement officials we came to call 'goons' pretty hard to swallow. They'd come up to you and tell you what to do quite aggressively, although they'd rock back on their heels a bit when you replied, as Kiwis tend to do, 'Who the hell are you?'

For all this, though, Iran has some advantages over other countries we traversed. Women have equality of employment opportunity and equal pay. The workforce is very well educated, although many leave for the West as a consequence. Jo was a major hit with the women who, clearly chafing under the regime but too scared to do it themselves, encouraged her to defy the dress code and cheered her on wherever we went. There was plenty of fascination here, too, about how one woman managed with so many rough-looking husbands. One woman whom Jo met was heavily pregnant, and disgustedly showed her the layers of clothing she was obliged to wear, the 30-degree heat notwithstanding. And we saw the same thing in our hotels, where the domestic staff were kitted up like medieval nuns, never mind the bending and kneeling and hard physical work their jobs entailed.

All in all, given the palpable lack of respect in the general population for the oppressive rule of the fanatical clerics, you get the impression that Iran is between revolutions just now.

We had one particularly hard day when we decided to take an alternative route to a mountain village named Masuleh. Access was by a rough dirt road, and Mansuer couldn't follow. He anxiously extracted a promise from us to rendezvous with him at the hotel by a certain time, and we set off. The road just kept on getting worse, turning to deep, greasy mud. We all had our moments where we thought we were off. Some of us had our moments where we *were* off. The thick mud had clogged the tread of our tyres, turning them into slicks. Ruts can be tricky. On a heavy bike, such as one laden with gear, you slow down, but still the slippy-slideys can get the better of you.

Phil came off. Jo came upon him standing beside his bike massaging his wrists. He'd been heading downhill into a corner and just couldn't get enough strength in his grip to get the brakes and clutch on.

'I can't stand the bike up,' he said.

'I can't do it on my own either. But no worries. Brendan's coming,' Jo replied. Eventually Brendan arrived and, with his expertise at righting trailbikes, Phil was soon back up.

Then we decided we were lost. Bryan came back from up ahead and reported that the road had finished. We all scoffed, and Brendan rode on to see for himself.

'You wouldn't call it a road,' he said, upon his return, 'but I reckon we can get through.' With plenty of slithering and sliding and carrying on, get through we did. We came down the hill and found ourselves on the wrong side of a barrier designed to stop people going up from Masuleh. The gatekeepers were bemused to see us. Where the hell, you could see them wondering, did *they* come from?

It ended up being quite a gruelling side-trip, but if we were glad to see the hotel at the day's end, our joy paled beside Mansuer's. He practically wept to see us, and probably would have kissed us one by one if we'd let him. He had clearly begun to think we'd given him the slip, and was beginning to contemplate the consequences.

Probably the highlight of the Iranian leg of our trip was the visit we made on May 14 to the Valley of the Assassins, of which Marco Polo wrote. The fortress of Alamut, which is still there, perched high on its mountain-top, was the centre of activities of the 11th-century Hashish-iyun sect, basically a bunch of Islamic mercenaries trained by a fanatical imam for freelance involvement in the Crusades. His method was to take young men and dose them with narcotics of various descriptions and let them loose in his heavily defended valley, which was a fully stocked, five-star pleasure garden, complete with hot-and-cold-running milk and honey and virgins — all the accoutrements of paradise. After a couple of weeks, long enough for them to get a taste for this kind of living, he removed them from the valley and from their narcotic supply. Finding themselves in military training camps, they were told that they'd been to paradise, and if they hoped to live again in the style to which they'd become accustomed there, they would need to distinguish themselves in battle. Happily, the imam could provide them with the opportunity to do just that. These feared, driven warriors were known as the Hashish-iyun, from which the English word assassin is derived.

The fortress of Alamut is reached by a long, arduous and slightly hair-raising climb. When you're up there, you feel like you're in a castle perched on the edge of the access road to the Remarkables skifield. It's deeply impressive. Phil chose this moment to reveal that he had vertigo, and didn't enjoy it as much as the rest of us. Jo made the descent aboard a rented donkey while Dave followed muttering, 'nice ass'.

Iranian towns posed their problems for the Silk Riders, mostly in the form of a profusion of erratically driven Hillman Hunters. The bigger the town, the more Hunters. And nowhere were there more Hunters, more erratically driven, than in the Iranian capital, Tehran. We'd been warned about Tehran. It was, according to most of our informants, including Phil, the most dangerous city in the world to drive in, let alone pilot a bike through. When we tried to protest that the traffic couldn't be worse than in India, people just shook their heads at us sadly. So it was with some trepidation we rolled toward Tehran on May 15. We fought our way, in full Wedgie formation, to a bus park on the outskirts of the city to await Mansuer, who was to escort us into the city to the Turkmenistan embassy to get our visas and then on to an inner-city hotel. He was there, bang on time. By ten in the morning we were following his car, complete with flashing lights. The scene that greeted us was horrendous. There were seven or eight lanes of traffic, everyone ducking and weaving across the carriageway with no regard for lane markings or indicating.

As we proceeded, the inevitable road lice appeared and latched onto our group, buzzing around us, infiltrating the Wedgie until they were persuaded to desist, laughing, waving, gesticulating wildly. By the time we neared central Tehran, there must have been 50 popgun bikes in our entourage.

Jo was in the lead, as close behind the guide car as she dared. Even so, Iranians kept cutting in front of her, or crowding close beside her, until she yelled at them to bugger off. If a woman on a motorbike was a novelty for the men of Tehran, then a shouting woman on a motorbike was positively unheard of. One old fellow must have admired her spirit, as he pulled right across in front of her and stopped, leaning out his window to ask whether she needed a husband. Jo gestured at the five bikers behind her and told him in no uncertain terms that she had more than she could handle already. Even as she was rejecting him, a bus gave her suitor the hurry-along with its front bumper. We got moving again as best we could.

Our stop–start progress through the traffic was again taking its toll on the bikes, which were overheating. As we were going through an unlit tunnel, Gareth's suddenly stalled and refused for the first little while to restart — not a particularly salubrious situation in the bedlam that is Tehran.

After the most full-on, demanding ride of our careers, we reached our first destination, the travel agency. Stopping gave the road lice and everyone else with normal levels of curiosity the chance to catch us up and get up close and personal. Pandemonium ensued. We were there for 20 minutes, and in that time we had the road police dealing with the rubberneckers travelling up the road on the wrong side, the cc police trying to confiscate our bikes, the scarf police haranguing Jo and trying to educate her in basic Islamic decency, and yet another group of uniformed officials wanting to see our passports. Then the army showed up. Thank god for the travel agency, who took the lead in negotiations with all interested parties at the same time as they were sorting out our Turkmenistan visas. We, meanwhile, lapped up the attention. Jo was showing her bike to a group of women in chadors, who were taking turns sitting on the saddle. Suddenly Mansuer, who seemed to have decided we were falling behind schedule, hurried up and gave the women a bollocking. They flinched as though he was about to hit them, and cowered. We made to intervene but they were already off, leaving Mansuer with his chest ridiculously puffed out, staring after them.

After the scene we'd created, it was something of an anticlimax when we arrived at the hotel and locked the bikes in the basement away from their hundreds of admirers. We regrouped in the lobby, our eyes sparkling, chattering excitedly. We had, after all, just biked through the most dangerous city in the world and survived. It was, the veterans amongst us agreed, just like India — only on speed.

This May 17 was a red-letter day in Iran, we learned, as it was on this historic day that the very last Paykan rolled off the production line. The Paykan (pronounced 'pecan', like the nut), which was the star of the Iranian private-car fleet, was nothing less than the Hillman Hunter, which lived on in Iran long after it faded from the memory of British Commonwealth motorists. The whole production line, it seems, was sold lock, stock and single-barrel carburettor to Iran when England's Rootes Group had finished with it. Assembled in

New Zealand by Todd Motors in the years when cars couldn't be had for love or money and Kiwis were automotive beggars rather than choosers, the four-door, economical and lively Hunter served us well. Then it was the Iranians' turn to make the best of it. In its Middle Eastern afterlife, the Hunter enjoyed a 30-odd-year production run, in which time millions of units were churned out. Sure, there were innovations — the incarnation that menaced us from all sides in Tehran was a 1600 cc, fuel-injected model — but still a Hunter. Not so long ago, we were told, a good 95 per cent of all the cars on Iranian roads were Paykans.

That evening, there was another surprise in store for us. The New Zealand embassy told us that a press conference had been arranged for us, complete with television crew beaming us onto Iranian national television!

There were about 20 journalists present, all sitting around a long table. The general thrust of the questions was predictable. 'What do you think of Iran and Iranian people?' they asked.

We were delighted to tell them we found Iran beautiful and fascinating, with a rich cultural and historical heritage, and the people friendly and hospitable. There was great tourist potential for the country, we felt.

We kept the emphasis as firmly as we could on ourselves and Marco Polo, avoiding getting into any potentially embarrassing comment on Iranian or international politics. Anything highbrow related to trade and industry we just deflected to Phil, the resident expert.

And what did we think of the controversy surrounding Iran's nuclear power plants?

Everyone looked at Gareth.

We came from New Zealand, Gareth replied, which is a country proud to be nuclear free and GE free. The only plants we had in

New Zealand were organically grown.

That neatly fudged the issue and surely, Gareth reasoned, would earn him Brownie points with Helen Clark – he's still waiting!

We had a long day the next day. First, there was round two of Tehran traffic to negotiate. Then, safely clear of Tehran, we said our farewells to Mansuer, who was leaving us. We had a long day, riding up to the Caspian Sea coast with the intention then of heading east to see the ancient ruins of Alexander's Wall, close to the border with Turkmenistan. Things didn't quite pan out as planned, however.

The weather turned against us in the mountains north of Tehran, and we had a demanding ride — especially Bryan, who was crook. Once we hit the coast, we began looking for accommodation. In the mid-afternoon, we roared into Babolsar, a little town on the Caspian Sea around 150 km northeast of Tehran. We had the usual clutch of road lice in tow, and the usual scenes of chaos ensued when we stopped. Phil, Brendan and Bryan went off to see whether they could find a place to stay or somewhere to pitch our tents. The rest of us were surrounded by something like a hundred people when suddenly a group of goons shouldered their way through the crowd. They were clearly out to give us grief. The first thing they tried was pointing to the bikes and declaring them illegal in Iran. We just laughed at them, and showed them the documents we were carrying that exempted the Dakars from the cc limits. They were doubtless used to the deference of the poor old Iranian population who languish beneath them and their kind. Our defiance only seemed to wind them up more. They demanded our passports — or, at least, they demanded Gareth and Phil's; they seemed to assume Jo wouldn't be carrying one. Our visas weren't in order, they tried to tell us. We ridiculed this, too: the visas were fine, we told them, and what's more, they were written in Farsi. Anyone who could read Farsi — the official language of Iran — could surely see they were in order.

Well, that was more than they could take. Our passports were pocketed. They insisted we accompany them to their bleak-looking headquarters, and it was only when we saw this grim edifice — more like a New Zealand gang pad than anything else, complete with high, iron fence and gaggle of hoods adorning its steps and entranceway — that we began to realise we might be out of our depth here. Suddenly, we missed Mansuer.

When confronted by the unreasonable demands of authority or bureaucracy, the Iranian way, like the Latin way, is to deploy a kind of kinetic charm, waving your hands around and rolling your eyes beseechingly at the heavens, lamenting the difficulties that Allah (who is great) puts in the way of hard-working, humble folk. There's a pretty good chance that Mansuer, a professional tour guide and a master of the subtle arts of appeasement, could have talked us out of this situation. As it was, we lacked his charm and, just as crucially, the temperament just to play along with the goons. So here we were, arguing with the dangerously provoked petty tyrants of an Iranian backwater. The big cheeses disappeared inside while we waited, hoping we weren't going to be made to follow. To our immense relief, they emerged again and told us we were going to be taken to a 'hotel' while the alleged irregularities with our visas were ironed out.

They refused to let us call anyone, or even to wait for the others. For a while it looked as though we were going to be kept separated. In the end, though, we were deposited in the seedy-looking motel the others had lined up for us to stay in that night, and in which Bryan was already installed, having gone straight to bed. The goons saw us into our rooms and made a big show of locking the gates.

We wasted no time getting onto the New Zealand embassy and our local travel agent. Gareth may have earned a few Brownie points as a New Zealand cultural ambassador in the recent press conference, but he doubted it would be enough to interest Helen Clark in springing him from Iranian custody. Phil, on the other hand, was chairman of Trade and Enterprise and therefore valuable. We put the matter in his hands, and he'd soon mobilised pressure on the Iranian embassy in New Zealand. We enjoyed hearing him talking to the New Zealand embassy in Iran. He listened to something he was being told, then replied: 'Well, the version you have been given is considerably at variance with the facts. Let me tell you what's going on . . .'

Meanwhile, of course, the story was breaking in the New Zealand media. Gareth had managed to get through to Paul Holmes on his radio show by satellite phone — the producer was only too happy to patch him through when he heard what was going down — and he described our predicament, slightly gilding the lily by referring to our accommodation as a rat-infested hovel. All the attention doubtless helped the Iranians in Wellington to focus as they picked up the phone to talk to Tehran.

We learned that some kind of alterations might be necessary for our visas, so Jo sent hers down to the police station. We were getting pretty hungry. Sinister-looking Hillman Hunters crammed with thugs wearing dark glasses were cruising by on the hour and conspicuously counting our bikes. We decided to use the repressive female dress-code to our advantage. Jo decked herself out in full chador and went out looking for a shop and an internet café, with the motel owner driving. While he went foraging for food, she went to the internet café — the only woman in there — so she could alert the outside world to our predicament. We had no real idea what level of information was getting out beyond official circles, so she emailed son Sam back in New Zealand just in case he didn't hear of our troubles.

The food they brought back helped a little, but none of us were very happy. We'd been in Iran for ten days, and to say we were missing booze is an understatement. The closest we'd come was when Jo had located a few tins of what looked like Turkish beer. It had the name

— Efes — on the can, but the fine print, which was in Arabic script, would have alerted us, had we been able to read it, that this was 'malt drink'. It was unspeakably disgusting. Bryan's immunity seemed to be indexed to his sobriety, so he had come down with the bug that had previously hit Jo and Gareth. Phil's carpal tunnels were giving him arseholes, and he was just about cross-eyed with the need for a drink. It was Phil, of course, who had urged us not to go along with the sly-grogging schemes that had been offered to us here and there along the way. You don't get a slap on the wrist for defying the laws of Iran, he pointed out. You lose the wrist altogether.

Brendan's behaviour had been causing concern for some days now: he'd been riding off by himself muttering incoherently, and now, with no booze and under house arrest, Dave's seemingly irrepressible sense of humour was quite definitely repressed. The most violent — or at least, colourful — reaction of all to our enforced spell of temperance was Gareth's. One morning, Jo came down to breakfast and announced that Gareth's privates had gone orange. Had anyone else's gone orange, she wanted to know. No, everyone else had retained their natural colouring. The only explanation we could think of was that it was all the vivid orange Fanta Gareth had been drinking in lieu of alcohol.

As we sat in the seedy Babolsar motel, the irony — that we had only hours before been extolling the virtues of Iran as a tourist destination to a mass television audience — was not lost upon us.

After a night listening to Gareth's imaginary rats scratching around in the motel walls, we learned the difficulties had been ironed out. The policeman who arrived to give us the news presented us with a letter of introduction and a list of contacts at Babolsar Police in case we had any further trouble this side of the border with Turkmenistan. He insisted that Jo cover her head more effectively — her Icebreaker beanie was not up to scratch — and, with a flourish, unlocked the gates to the motel. Free at last, oh lord. We had breakfast, and the people staying in the neighbouring motel unit — Iranians — brewed up a cup of tea for us in their Thermette. Then Jo went off for a dip in the Caspian — in full chador, of course. Try as she might to be culturally sensitive and compliant — she even tried riding in it, a sight to behold — she just couldn't quite seem to manage to make the grade. A man advised her that her face and head cover were fine: it was her bottom that was getting her into trouble. It turns out that the chador has to conceal the *shape* of a woman's body as well as cover it.

Whether because Balbosar's finest had phoned ahead or because we were beneath the radar of the remaining petty bureaucracies whose paths we crossed, we had no further problems in Iran. We reached the border with Turkmenistan thoroughly in love with the Iranian people — and thoroughly loathing the authorities. Nice place to visit, but you wouldn't want to live there. We were all pretty happy to leave. Phil in particular, who'd clearly been wrestling with demons from his time living there, was elated.

Anyone for desert?

That far into a trip like this, you start missing your personal space. We tended to have a beer and hang out together in the evenings after each day's ride, but not necessarily, and not necessarily everyone at once. Even when the group was together, we'd tend to find ways of closing ourselves off, whether tapping away on our i-mates sending emails and texts, or firing up our music. Four of us — Gareth, Jo, Brendan and Bryan — had iPods, and getting one of these out was a signal you wanted a bit of time out. Gareth spent a lot of time in his own little musical world, thanks to his iPod. Jo, on the other hand, discovered early on that the act of putting on the headphones alone was enough to get some peace, whether or not she played music though them. Together alone: it's the only way a trip like this could ever work.

We'd already been riding for a couple of hours from Bojnurd in northeastern Iran by the time we reached the collection of dusty buildings that marked Gaudan, and the border with Turkmenistan. And it had been hard going — narrow, winding mountain passes that demanded all your concentration and a readiness to veer toward the shoulder at the sudden appearance of the wildly veering local traffic. We'd had a stop in Bajgiran, a small town just on the Iranian side of the border, where a group of young men had made us very welcome in whatever combination of pidgin English and hand gestures they could contrive. They'd seen tourists before, they told us. Last year. And they were very happy we had come.

Again, it was compulsory to have a guide through Turkmenistan, although this time it was a direct requirement of the government rather than being a disguised tariff as in Iran, where if you don't buy some tourist 'services' you can't procure an invitation to visit. So we met Sanja, the guide laid on by Silk Road Adventures, at the border. He was a pleasant, rotund sort of fellow, and a bit of a relief after Mansuer, even if we felt he could have been a little more proactive in helping with the border formalities. After Iran, we had resigned ourselves to a long, belligerent wrangle with bureaucracy at the border, but to our surprise the uniformed personnel manning the desks were pleasant, well presented and made no mention of 'tourist tax' or other such inducement. They were friendly and shook hands with us at the completion of every step in the (admittedly lengthy) process. There was very little traffic, and everything we needed — chiefly the offices of the innumerable branches of Turkmen bureaucracy — was close at hand, easily within walking distance. It took a while — five hours, give or take — but the processes seemed coherent, intelligible and orderly. We were impressed.

From the crossing point, it was an easy half-hour ride down to Ashgabat, the capital of Turkmenistan, perched on the edge of the Karakum Desert. After the dusty, muddy streets of eastern Iran, with the abject adobe housing, riding into Ashgabat was a surreal experience. Sure, we had read that Turkmenistan was a resource-rich country, with huge oil reserves under the Caspian Sea and on-shore natural gas fields, and that now its wealth was no longer being siphoned off by its former master, the Soviet Union, it was pretty well-to-do. And sure, we thought things would be a bit different out from under the oppressive regime of the Iranian mullahs. But none of us expected the spectacle that greeted us.

Out of the desert rears a huge archway. You pass underneath, wondering what in hell that's in aid of, when all of a sudden Ashgabat appears before you, its modern-looking skyline shimmering in the heat mirage. It only got more fantastical the nearer we drew. Huge, ultra-modern office and apartment buildings flanked the streets, which were lined with trees and fountains. Fountains were everywhere, in open defiance of the desert on the city's doorstep. It was like Las Vegas, except bigger and more thoroughly given over to water features. We stared about ourselves, agog. After the chadors of Iran, the colourful floral prints and simple headscarves the women wore seemed unimaginably modish and revealing. Jo enjoyed the clothes, while the boys enjoyed the comparative lack of them.

Our hotel, the Nissa, had been prearranged for us. While Turkey and Iran had eroded our expectations, we couldn't quite believe our luck when we checked in. It was all marble and chrome and — yes — water features, including a pool and a Turkish steam-bath, and quiet, but for the cool whisper of air conditioning. We were delighted by certain water features: our rooms even had proper toilets.

Just about our first stop, of course, was the hotel bar. After ten days of enforced teetotalism in Iran, we had a powerful thirst to slake. The staff seemed quite familiar with this phenomenon. Turkmenistan receives about 20,000 visitors a year, they told us, and the worst tourists by far are the Iranians, who slip across the border now and then to go on a sneaky bender. The other clientele were mostly Russians, middle-aged men surrounded by young women with the slender figures of supermodels and the faintly professional air of prostitutes. The women eyed us up as we arrived, their stares lingering on the boys and barely registering Jo. Jo spoke to one of the men at some point in the evening, and the woman he was with did everything but arch her back and hiss like a cat. There was some serious turf-infringement going on. As far as Jo was concerned, they were welcome to one another.

We spent the following day wandering around downtown Ashgabat. We attracted the (as it seemed) inevitable attention from the authorities, this time for merely taking photographs. We were snapping the huge, opulent, ostentatious palaces which line the streets when a carload of goons in uniforms pulled up and tried to confiscate our cameras. This was a reminder that we were still in a state struggling to shrug off its despotic past — as if any were needed, besides the gargantuan posters of Saparmurat Niyazov, otherwise known at his own insistence as 'Turkmenbashi' (beloved leader of all the Turkmens), the former Soviet henchman who clung onto power when the USSR fell apart in the 1990s. These were everywhere, along with Turkmenbashi-themed statues and fountains. Dave showed them a carefully edited selection of pictures on the viewfinder of his digital camera to convince them that we weren't photographing the palaces. This appeased one lot, but just around the corner was another bunch, who again were anxious to relieve us of our cameras. Idiotically though, when we asked whether they would take a photograph of us, they were happy to oblige, even though we were posed with one of the forbidden palaces in the background.

On television that night, we saw the self-proclaimed great man himself in a local version of reality TV. There he was, reclining on a bed of roses, explaining to three of his cowering ministers why he was sacking them. This, we learned, was a regular ritual, apparently designed to show the general population how staunchly anti-corruption the great leader is. After all, they need a bit of convincing. Niyazov runs the country more or less single-handedly and, predictably, almost totally for his own gain. The average wage (in that part of the economy which functions on money) is US$150 per month, but all electricity, petrol, iodised salt, telephone and postal services are free to Turkmens. This, at least, is the theory. When we visited a petrol station, we found a long, stoic queue waiting at the single bowser (out of six) that was actually dispensing fuel. The Turkmen people are accustomed to queuing: it was par for the course under Soviet rule, and while communism has supposedly packed up and gone, you'd be hard-pressed to see the difference in anyone's daily lives.

The State still predominates. Government employees receive discounts to buy houses — anything up to 50 per cent. The government employs well over half the paid workforce. A compulsory military service regime is in force, and every young man gets to spend a couple of years in the army, mostly on guard duty around the numerous monuments to the president.

The next day, we made preparations to set off on a side-trip from the Silk Road, a visit to the heartland of Turkmenistan and in particular the Aral Sea. Most Turkmens we talked to thought we were mad to venture out there. The Karakum Desert covers roughly 80 per cent of their country's land area, but the town-dwellers never go there if they can help it. They call it 'the black desert', not because of the colour of its sand (which is cream through white), but because of the range of untoward things said to befall those who attempt to traverse it. People were vague about the precise nature of the threat, but it seems Turkmens are raised on blood-curdling tales of mystical misadventure and of mishaps of a more conventional kind, usually involving bandits.

We weren't taking it lightly, either. It was a round trip of 1200-odd kilometres, and the temperature was supposed to range from around zero at night to the mid-40s during the day. We were warned to up-end our boots each morning before we put them on, to remove the scorpions.

There was very little on our route in the way of towns or even gas stations, so it was probably a good thing we had Sanja along in his support vehicle to carry our supplies. He brought a mate with him, a Turkmen-domiciled Russian, and between them they saw the vehicle was stocked with the necessaries — bottled water, of course, and petrol. Sanja presented us with the bill. We thought there must have been some mistake when we read the price of the 70 litres of petrol we had on board. But no, he shrugged, there was nothing wrong: 70 litres, 7000 manat (local currency) — a little over two New Zealand dollars! You've heard of the phrase 'cheap as water': well, fuel was a lot cheaper in Turkmenistan than the bottled water.

We set off a little after eight, and the superb roads of Ashgabat soon degenerated to a poxy tarsealed strip interrupted by sections of rutted track, which themselves gave way to lengths of sandy path through the desert. The massive potholes and crisscrossing of the tarseal strip with deep drifts of windblown sand were sufficient to keep us focused. Sporadically, the wind whipped up a little sandstorm and all but obscured the way forward. The temperature soared — as did our pulse rates every time a truck appeared through the shimmering heat mirage, its engine roaring and its transmission whining as it swayed and slewed all over the show in the soft sand. Here and there we came across upturned trucks, casualties of the fight to coax transport along this fragile link between Iran and the northwest corner of Uzbekistan. Broken-down Soviet-made Ural motorcycles littered the side of the road, too, a cautionary reminder to anyone not aboard a BMW — or so we hoped.

Our training in the Australian outback began to stand us in good stead, as we applied the techniques we had perfected there. The trick in soft sand is to get your weight as far back over the back wheel as you can (not easy when you've got gear piled up behind you) and, contrary to your instincts, to apply more power, because the faster you go, the less likely your front wheel is to deflect from your track and plough in sideways. Nevertheless, there were a few sand flops. Jo's bike, with smaller wheels and wider tyres, was giving more trouble than the others. Brendan watched her critically, offering advice, and at one point offered to take her bike through a difficult patch, an offer that she appreciated but — Jo being Jo — declined. It wasn't long before she had the knack of it.

The other trick with the BMWs, however — and we weren't always onto this one — is to disengage the active-braking system when you're about to enter soft riding conditions. You'd be riding along and see everyone stopped and wonder what the hell for. Well, with our bikes, you had to stop and hold down a button as you restarted them to disengage ABS. Active-braking systems work by sensing loss of traction in the rear wheel and reducing the amount of braking power until it is re-established. This is all fine and dandy on hard surfaces, such as an asphalt road, where loss of traction in the rear wheel means a wheel locking up and a skid about to happen. In sand or deep gravel, however, it just means you're in sand or deep gravel. So what you find, if ABS is still engaged, is that you're heading down a sandy slope applying the back brakes and they're not working. The end result is palpitations at least and more often than not a very untidy finish. So after a dicey moment or two, we learned pretty quickly to take the ABS off when it looked soft ahead. Everyone except Brendan, that is: since the ABS only applied to the rear brakes, this trailbike maestro, for whom the front brake is everything, didn't even notice the difficulties.

After trial and error, we had hit upon the ideal combination of clothes with which to stay cool. You could strip the Gore-Tex lining out of your riding jacket to lighten it and make it cooler. If you wanted, you could leave only the mesh lining inside, but the drawback with this is that if you have a spill, the mesh burns your skin quite badly. Gareth found wearing an Icebreaker merino top with full sleeves, soaked with water, underneath his jacket really lowered his temperature, trapping the water next to his skin and cooling it as it evaporated. Jo followed suit, and so did a couple of the others. Dave, on the other hand, couldn't imagine how a thermal woollen undershirt could possibly do anything other than help you fry. It wasn't until he tried the trick on a trip in outback Australia after the Silk Road adventure that he became a convert.

It's funny how much life there is in what appears at first to be an inhospitable wasteland: all you need to do is stand still for long enough and you'll see it. Shortly after we got out into the wilderness proper, Jo thought she spotted a dusty landmine at the side of the road. She stopped and turned off her bike, only to see the 'mine' sprout a long, leathery neck and four legs and amble off. Who'd have thought you'd see a tortoise in the desert? And Gareth was squatting in answer to a call of nature off to the side of the road when he noticed several strange creatures converging on him from among the surrounding rocks and stubble. There were a couple of dozen of them: long, reddish bugs with front nippers to shame the paddle crabs back in Oriental Bay. They were making a beeline for him but he kept them at bay by showering them with handfuls of gravel, happy when he stoned the occasional one to death. It wasn't until some time afterward that he mentioned the experience, whereupon he was assured that these were scorpions, and he was lucky none of them had hitched a ride in his trousers.

The comparison with the Australian outback was irresistible, but there was one important difference. People are sparse in the outback. In the Karakum, by contrast, many do their best to farm it. Nowadays, the bulk of Turkmenistan's population either cool their heels in the fountains in Ashgabat if they're on the government payroll, or live on the outskirts of one of the oasis towns in the southern Karakum Desert. But there are still a good few who live the traditional Turkmen nomad's lifestyle, drifting about the arid interior with a herd of goats and a camel in tow to carry their yurt. It must be an incredibly hard life. Nevertheless, Jo found something to envy: she wished she had extra luggage space so she could buy some of the incredible clothes the nomads wear. At the very least, she resolved, she would score one of those big, shaggy Turkmen hats.

As the day wore on, clouds piled up over the horizon and treated us to spectacular displays of lightning and thunder. We stopped in mid-afternoon and broke out the tents, just as a fierce wind whipped up and tried to carry away both the tents and the big tarpaulin we wanted to sit on. After a struggle, we made a little Fairydown city for the night, complete with blazing fire to warm the weary cockles of our hearts. The first raindrops fell just after dark, and thereafter it pissed down: the equivalent of five years' rainfall, we were assured by our guide, in one night.

The next day, as we neared the Uzbek border, we began to see more signs of life. Irrigation had enabled the farmers to coax something green — principally cotton and grain — from the desert here and there. The effort to take water from the Aral Sea and the rivers that feed it began long before the Mongols occupied this part of the world in the 12th century. Indeed it can be traced back to the second millennium BC and has continued sporadically ever since. It intensified under the Soviets, who embarked on an orgy of canal-building. There are canals and pipelines crisscrossing the desert every which way and with varying results.

The Soviet schemes might have been on a grand scale, but they were hardly the most efficient. Most of the water is conducted along unlined, open canals. We found ourselves riding alongside these for hundreds of kilometres, seeing their water seeping and evaporating into the desert every inch of the way. In places, we crossed uncultivated bogs, which petered out into desert metres away. Where the land was worked, the crops looked poor, promising low yields, for whereas these plots used to be worked by state-funded collectives, their productivity enhanced with subsidised fertilisers and insecticides, they are now owned and worked by individuals with no capital whatsoever to invest. Meanwhile, the salinity of the soil is rising as the irrigated water evaporates.

The people, needless to say, are poor, and dance to a tune composed by the Turkmen bureaucracy. The costs of their input are dictated by the middlemen who control distribution and add their own fat margins, while there is a single state-owned purchaser of their output that pays them well below what their produce fetches for the state on the world market — shades, Gareth was heard to mutter, of the New Zealand Dairy Board. It's a treadmill designed to yield hefty surpluses for the president and his lackeys, with the scraps used to subsidise the petrol, electricity, phones and postage of the predominantly urban population. The most poignant symbol of the absurdity of the Turkmen regime was all the water dripping, pouring and spraying from the fountains of Ashbagat while towns hundreds of kilometres closer to its source — the tributaries of the Aral — had no running water at all.

We spent our last night on Turkmen soil in the ancient town of Konye-Urgench on May 23, getting a glimpse of a few Polo-era relics, including some Islamic mausoleums and the tallest minaret in Central Asia, built in 1320. We crossed the border with relatively few hiccups the following day, and met the new guide (another example of tourist 'services' required to procure a letter of invitation) at Shavat.

As we got going, you could immediately see an improvement in the standard of living of the people. There was a more productive look about the land, with even machinery — albeit clapped-out, Soviet-era contraptions — working alongside the peasants with their hoes and sacks of seed. Every now and then you'd see a tractor that was less than ten years old, but not often. Uzbek agriculture was a cut above Turkmenistan, but light years below what New Zealanders would consider thriving.

We stayed overnight in Nukus, a few kilometres over the border. We learned from our guide that Nukus, population 200,000, was the principal site for the Soviet chemical-warfare effort, and the townsfolk blithely lived their lives in the shadow of factories producing some of the most toxic substances known to man. This is an indication of how much regard the Soviet regime had for the Uzbeks. Nor has the threat altogether gone away. Until recently, teams of American experts have been trying to clean up the mess, and some level of contamination will be there for a long, long time to come.

One of the features of butchers' shops in Uzbekistan — indeed, right across Central Asia — is the peculiar method they have of advertising the freshness of the meat they are selling to their customers. Outside the shop, you'd commonly see the four feet of a camel, or even a camel's head, which prospective customers would examine closely, peering at the soles of the feet, or peeling back the lips to look at the mouth and teeth. If they were satisfied with what they saw, they could go inside and buy a hunk of the same beast from the dismembered carcass hanging up within.

We had an early morning the next day, out of deference to Phil's intolerance of the heat. It was a long, demanding ride to the Aral Sea, and the temperature soared by midday to 48 degrees Celsius.

The Aral Sea is fed by a number of streams and rivers but, at their zenith, the two principal ones, the Amu-Darya river flowing from the Hindu Kush in Afghanistan and the Syr-Darya from Kyrgyzstan, would have made the Waikato look like a dribble. Right along their length, however, they have been tapped to feed irrigation, and today they are just muddy trickles upon their arrival at the Aral. Consequently — and famously — the Aral has been in full retreat for decades, and now covers only 70 per cent of its glory-days area.

Our destination there was Moynaq, the southern of the Aral's two main fishing ports. The town is still home to around 3000 people, but we wondered how long they can hang on there. The sea shore is now 40 km away, and we had all seen those iconic *National Geographic* shots that showed Moynaq's fishing fleet parked high and dry on the salty, scrubby shingle just off the dusty, dry jetty. Our guide assured us that there was nothing of the sort to be seen today, although we weren't convinced he was on the level. He seemed to find the whole question somewhat embarrassing.

The town, needless to say, has itself hit rock bottom. Much of the population has found other things to do than fishing, but to all appearances, none of it has really paid off. Moynaq is a filthy, squalid little place, and several of the children we saw had skin diseases.

There was no shortage of children around, all dressed up in their best clothes. School had just broken up for the year, and they swarmed around us — and more particularly around our bikes, which we left on the roadside when a local we asked about the stranded boats pointed out a dusty track. While we wandered out to photograph the marooned vessels on the dry seabed, the kids were busily playing with the controls and rummaging through our panniers. They scattered when we arrived, cursing, to shoo them away, but they were surging along the streets as we rode through them, to the point where a local policeman stopped us to warn us not to run over any children. He must have read our minds.

From the highest point of the elevated land on which Moynaq is situated, we could see a pall of black smoke billowing from the low outline of Vozrozhdeniya Island, which is fast becoming a peninsula. This, Captain Bryan told us, was where the Soviets had their main biological warfare facility; the smoke was a by-product of the plant which was busily destroying the stockpiles of lethal agents held there against the day the island becomes part of the mainland.

We believed him — for a while.

Half-biked

As we headed south through Uzbekistan, we were nearing the halfway point in our trip. The stresses and strains were beginning to tell on man and machine. Dave and Jo, who was all but over her cold by now, were initially spared the indignity afflicting the rest of us. Marco Polo spoke of the constant 'purging' he suffered in this region, mostly from drinking unsound water. We came to know the same phenomenon well, although by the name of 'the Silk Road squirts.' Of course, having travelled in Third World countries before, we took all sensible precautions. The general rule is that you eat what the locals eat, purify your water and so far as possible keep your hands clean. We were carrying General Ecology First Need Deluxe water filters, which eliminate everything larger than the smallest virus; we used antibacterial handwash and we steered clear of any, even bottled, water if we didn't know exactly what its provenance was. But no matter how careful you are, you're bound — or should that be unbound — to succumb sooner or later.

The Silk Road squirts tended to strike very shortly after you'd had a roadside meal. The food would look and smell really good, taste nice and go down well, but no sooner were you back up and riding than your guts would begin issuing urgent messages that you should prepare to jettison it. Depending on the severity of the disagreement within, you can find yourself with precious little time to obey before nature asserts itself.

Many was the time where, just after lunch, you'd come round a bend and find two or more bikes standing forlornly at the roadside with their riders either squatting beside them (urgent cases) or (non-urgent) running full pelt across an adjacent field or out of sight altogether in search of privacy.

Your dignity is an early casualty. In the initial stages of your affliction, you imagine you can contain the angry rumblings, the convulsive griping, and maybe relieve the pressure with a discreet gaseous emission or two, pending a convenient time and place to undertake a more substantial alleviation. This is a high-risk strategy. Too often that little gaseous intent turns out to be a full-blown liquid burn-off, and you find your motorcycle trousers are the hapless recipient of the exorcism your body just conducted on the demons of your lunch.

After a few such mishaps, you learn to recognise when you've fallen foul of food and to appreciate how time is then of the essence. You learn, as the song says, to know when to hold 'em, know when to fold 'em and, most definitely, when to run. Trouble was, if you found yourself running to a Central Asian public convenience, your trials were not necessarily over. Most New Zealanders left communal public toilets behind when they played their last game of footy at one of the rougher clubs. In the parts of the world traversed by the Silk Road, the toilets make the worst changing-room bogs you've ever seen look like the facilities at a five-star Hilton. You're usually confronted with a long gutter or drain, with a line-up of locals squatting there, each with a jug of water in front of him for the clean-up. You arrive, ripping your spacesuit off and gesturing to them to make room. This cheek-by-bowel experience requires you to back into whatever space there is, for all the world like reversing a trailer up to the edge at a landfill transfer station. Perched there with your roll of Purex in your hand, you present far too rich a spectacle for the locals to let you get on with your business. Before you know it, they're all on their feet, staring at you curiously. No matter how urgent the need that brought you here, it becomes kind of hard to respond under these circumstances.

Between toilet stops, we admired Uzbekistan and its people. We had been the recipients of incredible generosity wherever we went, but it reached new heights among the Uzbeks. We'd have the greatest of difficulty getting roadside vendors to take money from us: giving us their wares was the least they could do, they indicated to us, to requite the honour we'd done them by stopping at their stall. We were mightily impressed, too, at the enterprise they showed. There are literally millions of micro-enterprises in evidence: every family, from the youngest child to the oldest granny, is helping to run one or more businesses. A typical family kept a few cows or goats, ran a roadside stall selling soft drinks, fruit or honey, touted their car or tractor for hire and baked bread to sell from a barrow they pushed through the streets.

There was a fleeting hope when Uzbekistan finally slipped the collar of Soviet domination that the nation would be able to capitalise on all this entrepreneurialism. And so they would have, were it not for Islam Karimov, who installed himself as the traditional post-Soviet bully-boy leader and chief beneficiary of the Uzbek economy. Whenever a business begins to get ahead, it receives a visit from Karimov's 'associates', who inform its directors that it is now the property of the Uzbek state, viz Karimov and his family. 'State-owned' businesses enjoy fantastic incentives from the regime: practically every car you see in Uzbekistan, for example, is a Daewoo, ever since Karimov's daughter received the Daewoo agency and the government slapped a

100 per cent tariff on other makes and models.

There are two sad, predictable consequences of this kind of nonsense. First, while it prevails, there is no chance that Uzbekistan will attract the kind of foreign investment it needs to make the jump from a subsistence economy to anything capable of delivering a better way of life to its people. At present, the agricultural sector is little removed from the Soviet model, with most of the farms still owned and worked by collectives. Each day, as we set out on the road, we saw peasants trudging, tools over their shoulders, to the fields for a day's back-breaking manual work.

Second, history suggests that like most thug-rulers, Karimov will not be persuaded to give up power without a fight, and probably a bloody one at that. The Uzbeks are too busy trying to keep food on the table to bother much about the regime, but that situation won't last forever. And while Karimov has so far managed to keep a lid on Islamic 'extremism' by sheer, brute force — 90 per cent of the 26 million Uzbeks are Muslim — by keeping people in such a state of deprivation, he only makes the resurgence of Islamic fundamentalism inevitable. When you hear of Uzbekistan in the West, it tends to be in the context of the coming revolution. Certainly the signs are there. Just before we arrived, a civilian protest in the town of Andijan, close to the Kyrgyz border, was brutally suppressed by the army. And you can't get local currency for love or money — or, at least, not from a bank. After all, the bank's the last place you'd want your hard-won savings languishing when the revolution comes. People hoard all their sum (the local currency) at home. We had to use American dollars in the hotels. We did manage to get hold of a few sum after queuing and paying a margin, from a man running a black-market exchange. We learned later that we were taking a big risk doing this, as it is against the ruthlessly enforced laws of Karimov's beleaguered regime.

The Uzbeks have always had problems with politicians. Our trip took us through four of the region's ancient khanates — the little kingdoms overrun by the Mongols in the 12th century. The Mongol tyrants, the khans, were all pretty rugged individuals, but none was perhaps quite so nasty as the khan of Khiva. Our guide tried to collect money off us for the privilege of looking around Khiva but we left one of our number, ostensibly to negotiate with him, while the rest wandered off. At a given moment, the negotiations were broken off, and the negotiator joined the rest. The guide, meanwhile, was left to explain to whoever ran the guiding racket why he had allowed these Kiwi bikers to cheat the system. Like many of the officials we dealt with on our Silk Road adventure, this fellow didn't seem that sorry to see the back of us when we left.

We enjoyed Khiva, an ancient, walled city which the Soviets restored to be a 'living museum' of the glory days of the Mongol empire. Perhaps it's a quirk of the biker personality, or merely our particular personalities, but all six of us got a real kick out of viewing the torture chambers, complete with the torturer's tools of the trade, which were on display in Khiva. There were replicas of the bags they used to stitch you up in with a dozen wild cats if you'd pissed the khan off. There was a tower they biffed traitors off, their landing made all the more poignant by a forest of sharpened stakes. There was an instrument specially designed for gouging people's eyes out and— our particular favourite — another for slitting your face from ear to ear. This punishment was reserved for those who *really* pissed the khan off, whether by smoking or drinking or speaking out of turn. Perhaps he just liked being surrounded by wide smiles. Either way, we made a pact not to tell Garth McVicar of the Sensible Sentencing Trust about the khan of Khiva.

While it's a bit sterile and a little too like a theme park, Khiva made for a fascinating change from the crumbled ruins we had seen so far, where we'd had to use plenty of imagination to picture what they had been like at their zenith. Around 4000 people live there today, most of them dependent on tourism for their crust. The recent unrest in Uzbekistan had severely depleted tourist numbers: from 200,000 per annum, visitors have fallen away to around 17,000. The local people's loss was our (selfish) gain, as we were able to enjoy our tour in relative peace and quiet.

Uzbekistan is littered with relics of the Silk Road, their names resonating throughout Marco Polo's writings. The first we came across on our trip south from the Turkmen border was Urgench. It was the northernmost caravanserai for merchants moving to and from Russia; today, it's a dusty, water-starved town. And all around the Khiva region there are extensive archeological diggings. You'd be riding across featureless desert when you'd suddenly come across the fully exposed fortifications of settlements that were here long before the birth of Christ. Now that is humbling.

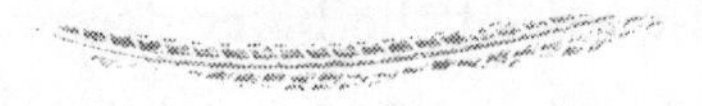

As we neared Bukhara in central Uzbekistan, it was noticeable that Brendan and Captain Bryan were pushing their bikes a little harder than Phil, Dave, Jo and Gareth — leaning into the corners a little more and opening up on the straights. Whenever we stopped for a break, they seemed impatient to hit the road again. It had, as noted earlier, been a long trip for all of us, but it was longer for the partnerless lads than for us. By the time we reached Uzbekistan, they were beginning to eye up the livestock in a way that wasn't altogether savoury, and definitely not encouraged by anything you'd find in the Koran. Fortunately we'd foreseen this phase of things, and had pencilled in what we called amongst ourselves the 'spousal arousal' tour. Caroline Keogh and Marion Wyness were flying in to join their hubbies for a spot of sightseeing, although it wasn't exactly sightseeing that Brendan and Bryan were looking forward to.

Just getting into Bukhara was an adventure. Gareth stopped at a roundabout on the outskirts and waved Jo through while he waited for the others. Each of the bikes passed, and then Gareth set off after them. It was a while before he found them and, meanwhile, they were all having trouble finding one another. We were all completely lost and separated for a while. Eventually, however, tired and grumpy, we found our separate ways to the hotel. The reunion of Brendan and Bryan with their wives was a little more touching than the moment where the Silkies finally caught up with one another.

While all that 'sightseeing' was going on, Jo had an adventure of her own in Bukhara. Late at night, as Dave, Gareth and Jo were wandering back to our digs, trying not to fall into the open drain in the narrow, high-walled street, a woman approached Jo and, in passable English, invited her to a nearby house for a cup of chai, the local tea.

Keen to see what lay behind the stone walls which leaned in over the streets, she readily assented. She accompanied the stranger to a doorway and they went inside.

Inside — wow! There was a courtyard luxuriantly planted with tomatoes, vines and herbs of all descriptions. Her host signalled to her to remove her shoes and wash her hands and then led her into the house. Directly inside, there was a large 'family room', complete with family — at least 30 people — seated on brightly coloured, silk cushions around a cloth laid out with all manner of food. Four generations were represented, along with friends, and all made a big fuss of her as she entered. Their grasp of English was about as extensive as Jo's command of Uzbek, but they managed to convey to her that someone was having a birthday and it would be rude if she didn't help them with their celebration, their meal and their vodka.

So she tried the assorted dried and fresh fruits, the cuts of cold meat, the yoghurts and the pastries and the huge variety of nuts and sweets. It was a gastronomic voyage of discovery, the colour, textures and tastes simply wonderful. Jo soon decided her favourites were the apricot and cherry preserves and the salami-style sausages powerfully redolent of garlic, but it was a close-run thing. Suitably fortified with food and a few vodkas — to the chagrin of her hosts, Jo sipped rather than knocked it back Uzbek-style — she sang happy birthday with the family clapping along, laughing and smiling.

Soon enough, the women insisted she get her *moosh* (husband) to join the party. Several of the teenagers escorted her to the hotel, but even once she'd shaken him awake and let him smell the quality of the vodka and the garlic sausage on her breath, Jo couldn't persuade Gareth to come. She went next door and said: 'Dave, there's a party down the road. You up for it?'

'You shouldn't be out there by yourself,' his muffled voice replied.

'Yeah, it's really dangerous and Gareth won't come,' Jo said.

There was a pause.

'Well, I suppose I'd better come and make sure you're all right,' he sighed.

Armed with a camera and a paua shell for the birthday boy, off they went. It took some doing, much laughter, blank stares and gesturing to convince the party that Dave was a friend, not her *moosh* — Jo soon learned the Uzbek phrase for 'yeah, right' — but *moosh* or friend, he was welcome. The floor was cleared and the local ladies danced with Dave and Jo and everyone danced with babies while teenagers hung in the windows, providing a disparaging commentary and laughing. Even the 55-year-old birthday boy was coaxed onto the floor to strut his stuff.

Jo and Dave wanted to stay all night, and the family did their best to make them. But with a 5 am departure for Samarkand in prospect, they had to get some sleep, so everyone said their farewells in the Uzbek style — kiss one cheek, then the other, then the first kiss again. Dave was clearly a hit. The 78-year-old matriarch of the family tearfully pressed him to stay forever so that she could teach him to drink vodka like a real man. He and Jo finally took their leave with an invitation to next year's birthday party ringing in their ears.

The next day, after an early start, it was on to Samarkand, with the Silk Riders on their steeds and the spousal party following in a car. Samarkand's very name is synonymous with the ancient Silk Road. It's a jewel of antiquity and, happily, everyone who's ever ruled the place has thought so, too. It's been preserved as close as you could hope for to its considerable romantic, mystical glory. It's beautifully kept: the streets are lined with trees that make it reminiscent, of all places, of Christchurch, only supposing Christchurch was full of mosques. The mosques, minarets and medrasses are huge and sumptuously decorated.

Samarkand contains reminders of yet another troublesome politician of yore, namely Tamerlaine, or Timur the Lame, who succeeded Genghis and Kublai Khan as the tyrant of tyrants of Central Asia. We visited his tomb. Timur may have been a genocidal maniac, but as far as the Muslims are concerned he was *their* genocidal maniac, so the locals are proud of him. They flock to his tomb to pay homage.

It was in Samarkand that we struck our first significant bike problem. So far, they'd been going beautifully, despite the hammering they were receiving. There were some minor niggles, and the mud deflectors at the back had self-dismantled on half the fleet, but it was all either cosmetic stuff or easily fixed. On May 30 Gareth was trying to kick his steed into life but it was being sullen. After a lengthy session of cranking, cursing and a bit of tinkering, it was clear this was no mere refusal to start. She wasn't even firing, which suggested an electrical fault. Between them, Brendan, Dave and Bryan diagnosed a problem with the starter solenoid. That was the easy part. The next, more demanding trick was fixing it.

Dave and Bryan went on a scouting mission to the Samarkand auto bazaar and returned triumphantly bearing a large cylinder from which wires dangled: the ignition switch from some Russian tank of a car — a Volga — they rather fancied. They performed a graft, in essence bypassing the ignition circuit in the way a generation of Kiwis grew up bypassing the ignition circuit of Ford Anglias whenever they lost their keys or failed to satisfy the usual criteria of ownership. It might have been a hot-wire, but it was an unbelievably sophisticated hot-wire, including a locking switch that was activated by a Volga key. Dave and Bryan completed the installation and tested it out. It worked a treat, but wasn't without its idiosyncrasies. They carefully explained to Gareth the new reality with which he would be living at startup time. He listened attentively, nodding now and then.

First disarm the bike alarm. Then turn the bike ignition switch on. Next — importantly — deactivate the bike kill switch and lift the bike sidestand. Then — more importantly still — ensure the bike is in neutral. Last, reach down to where we have mounted the Volga switch, directly adjacent to a certain sensitive part of your anatomy, and turn vigorously. Do everything in this sequence and, with a bit of fast cranking, she'd usually fire up fine.

We usually drew crowds when we were setting out, but never with quite the same air of anticipatory expectation as milled about Gareth from Samarkand onwards. Just what, you could see them wondering as he performed the Volga Manoeuvre, is he doing?

It was a complex procedure and Gareth, not at his best and sharpest after days of Marco Polo's 'constant, violent purging', struggled to keep his mind on the job. On a couple of memorable occasions, he forgot to ensure the bike was in neutral — easily done, because the solenoid fault meant the neutral light was on full time. What happened then was that as soon as he turned the Volga switch, the bike would fire and lurch forward. With the rider's hands otherwise occupied, it was out of control. The crowd, once they'd scrambled out of the way, never failed to roar their approval, clapping and laughing, while Gareth wrestled the bike under control and found neutral. You could sense their disappointment when he managed to get the bike going and pulled away, muttering his new mantra: 'Must remember to put the bike in neutral. Must remember to put the bike in neutral.'

Nor were our troubles at an end. On the way from Samarkand to Tashkent, Phil's bike began missing. We were all having trouble with the Uzbek fuel, which is only 72 octane and makes the motors pink like crazy. Phil pressed on, hoping it was something that could be thrashed back to health. But as the problem became noticeably worse, it was clear some investigation was needed. Dave and Bryan got to work, and thought they might have isolated the problem to an overly tight wiring harness. They adjusted this slightly, and the problem seemed to be fixed. We all fervently hoped it was. The bikes were due to receive their halfway service at BMW's Tashkent agency; so long as it made it, Phil's machine should be easily set to rights there. But nagging away at the back of our minds was the knowledge that Phil was finishing his half-Marco in Tashkent, and was due to hand over his steed to Selwyn, who was winging his way to Uzbekistan even as we listened to the roughly running motor and fretted. It was a long way to come to take over a non-functional motorbike.

Sure enough, about 100 km from Tashkent, the bike gave out altogether, cutting out and refusing to be restarted. Our resident experts, Brendan, Dave and Bryan, got to work on it. The mercury was pushing 45 degrees Celsius, and it had already been quite a long day. Jo volunteered to go on a drinks mission. She spied a café and turned off onto a dusty street, and next thing she knew, she was face-down in the gravel.

How the hell did that happen, she wondered.

She got to her feet, feeling pretty woozy, and went to try to get the bike back up. A couple of men came out from the café to help, and together they heaved the machine upright. The front wheel was stuck in a manhole, the cover of which had clearly flipped off when she hit it. The bike had stopped dead and she had sailed over the handlebars.

They had to drop the bike and slide it away from the hole before they could get it back on its feet.

Jo peered into her mirror to assess the damage. There was a small mark on her left cheekbone and it was very sore, but nothing seemed too seriously wrong.

Don't be a girl, she told herself.

Although she was still a little shaky, she completed her mission — buying food and drinks and taking it back to the boys. She kept her head down and didn't say anything about her little mishap, but after a while Gareth noticed that the left-hand side of her face had swollen up and was going several different shades of blue.

'What the hell happened to you?' he said.

The brains trust couldn't make any impression on Phil's bike, so we phoned ahead for a truck to come and fetch the machine and deliver it to BMW Tashkent. Phil told Jo that she was concussed, and should catch a lift on the truck with his dead bike while he rode hers the rest of the way in.

'Piss off,' she replied. 'You've broken your bike. You're not bloody riding mine.'

So off Phil went on the truck. As it turned out, all six bikes made the same assisted entry to the city as Phil's. Since the recent unrest, Karimov had declared the capital of Uzbekistan a motorcycle-free zone, since motorcycles were so convenient for guerillas performing drive-by shootings. We were met at a police station on the outskirts of the city by a truck, the bikes were loaded and all six were delivered to the workshop of Sanar Motors, the local BMW agent, this way.

At the hotel, Jo went straight to bed and fell deeply asleep, waking with a bad headache and bruising around both eyes and across the bridge of her nose. It had clearly been quite a spill after all. As team medic, she prescribed vodka for the pain, which seemed to do the trick. When we walked into the hotel bar, Jo noticed everyone was staring at her and, after a vodka-induced moment of vanity, realised it was out of admiration for the range of colours on her face and neck rather than lust.

Phil flew out shortly afterward. He was the surprise package of the group. For all the doubts that we might have had about him in the wake of the Australian shakedown trip, he proved to be a very valuable member of the team, not only in the tense situation in Iran, but in small ways right along the route. If anyone had had a particularly bad day, Phil would take them aside and pep them up a bit. And he developed a habit of putting fresh flowers, local grasses or whatever other curiosity he could find under the map cover on the tank of Jo's bike, a little detail she found herself missing after he had gone.

Taking his place was Selwyn Blinkhorne, whom we took to calling 'Phil-in'. He arrived to find, to his dismay, that his trip might be all over before it even began. It was a pretty tense time.

The following day, Dave, Bryan and Brendan got to work on the bikes. All were badly in need of the service we had planned on doing at Tashkent, but the most pressing issue was working out what was wrong with Phil's. Our resident mechanics knew more about the Dakars than the staff of Sanar Motors, who were more used to dealing with cars. The three of them fiddled and cursed while the rest of us hovered, making more or less stupid suggestions, until they lost patience with the unsolicited advice. Phil could act as gopher, they decreed. Jo should look after her injury. Gareth and Selwyn could just bugger off.

This superfluous duo wandered around the bazaars then made their way to an internet café where they sat drinking coffee and catching up on emails, waiting for the phone call for assistance that the pit crew were never quite desperate enough to make.

That evening, Dave and Bryan announced that they knew what the problem was with Phil's bike. It seemed it was a defect with the crankshaft position sensor, part of the new-fangled mechanism that has replaced the traditional breaker points and distributor in modern bikes. It was clearly a rare fault: BMW Tashkent didn't carry the spare; nor, it turned out, did Motorad back in New Zealand. We were going to have to get it delivered from BMW Munich, and that would take time.

Dave and Gareth convened a management meeting that evening, conscious that some hard decisions had to be made. Our entry date for China was non-negotiable. Any time lost in Tashkent would begin to crowd out the time we had allowed to travel the 1800 km to the Chinese border. If we eroded the 'headroom' we'd left ourselves to cope with any problems we might strike along the way — say, on the troubled border of Kyrgyzstan, or in the high mountain passes of that country — then we were asking for trouble. Because they had unmoveable arrangements on the other side of the Chinese border, the spouses would have to go on regardless of what we did.

But what, exactly, were we to do? There was clearly only one sensible decision to make. We couldn't all wait for the broken bike to be fixed. Two riders can move much faster than six. Four of us would go on, while Dave waited behind with Selwyn to effect the repairs to his bike. All going well, they'd race to catch us up before we crossed the Chinese border. Failing that, if he could wait no longer for the part to arrive, Dave would have to make the tough call: leave Selwyn behind to organise shipment of the bike back to New Zealand while Dave caught the group up on his own. Gareth was clearly concerned Dave's good nature would stand in the way of him making the call in time and he'd ruin his own trip. Some tense discussion followed. The person who stood to lose most, of course, was poor Selwyn, who hadn't ridden so much as a mile and yet was staring down the barrel of an early flight home if the spare didn't arrive in time or took too long to fit. But Dave's prospects were looking dicey also. Doing the 1800-km trip to the Chinese border, negotiating the various geopolitical hazards of Kyrgyzstan solo, was no mean undertaking. Any trouble en route, and the second half of his Marco was down the toilet, too.

Understandably, Selwyn had a bit of trouble accepting the plan. His situation was always going to be difficult, and we'd warned him about it before we even left New Zealand — walking into the group halfway through, when the team dynamics had all been sorted between us long ago. He was always going to feel on the outer. So there was probably as much of this at work as anything else when he accused Gareth of a lack of objectivity.

'If it was your bike,' he said to Jo, 'there's no way Gareth would've made this decision.'

Jo responded on the quiet: 'The bastard would, you know.'

Dave and Phil had a word to Selwyn, and while he was never exactly happy with it, there was nothing he could do. The plan stood.

In the meantime, Dave, Brendan and Bryan serviced the five functioning bikes, using a kit consigned by BMW Munich. Each got new tyres, courtesy of Metzeler. They may have gone out Metzeler's door free of charge, but by the time they arrived in Tashkent they'd acquired enough duty and assorted taxes to ensure we were paying a premium on the recommended retail anyway. But the value of fresh, new, quality tyres in this part of the world can hardly be overstated. We paid up gladly, happy to have them. Our experts were careful to perform the tyre changes manually themselves, anxious to avoid any damage an Uzbek mechanic might inflict to the rims in a moment of carelessness or using the wrong gear. We had a long way to go yet.

The service kits were supposed to contain an oil change for each of the bikes, too, but these had been intercepted somewhere along the way due to some obscure 'dangerous goods' regulations. That, at least, gave the lesser mechanical lights among us something to do: scour Tashkent for decent-quality motor oil.

One night, as we were strolling through the city, we came across a roadblock. Beyond it, the streets were empty. Suddenly, with a squeal of tyres, a line of black Chevvy Suburbans appeared, their windows rolled down and the barrels of machine guns protruding from every orifice. They roared along the wide downtown streets at something between 120 and 150 km/h, the internationally recognised standard speed for avoiding attack by rocket-propelled grenades. It was Karimov, of course, showing how great he felt his rapport with his people was these days.

On June 6, three days later than we'd planned, we finally hit the road again. It felt funny with only four of us. The other two glumly waved as we fired up our freshly serviced and sweetly running bikes. Selwyn looked pessimistic about his chances of seeing us again on this side of the world. Dave couldn't quite get into the mood even to make a crack about Jo's lopsided, technicoloured face. The two police cars we'd paid US$30 apiece to escort us out of the motorcycle-free zone turned on their flashing lights, and we fell in behind them. Soon we were doing a Karimov through the narrow, dusty streets of Tashkent, safe from RPG attack and finally appreciating what Helen Clark sees in this motorcade thing.

Kyrgyz courtesy call

It was around this time that we learned from email and from the Stuff website of the death in a motorcycling accident of Neil and Carol Bishop, a pair of New Zealanders who, together with a bunch of seven other motorcycle dealers, were touring in Turkey. We posted our condolences on the blog, and felt very much that there but for the grace of god went we. After all, each of us had our share of near-miss stories: with scarcely more than a whisker of miscalculation or a moment's inattention, or even a skerrick less luck, any one of these could have turned nasty.

Meanwhile, in New Zealand, people were hearing the news of two riders dying in Turkey. Many of our friends assumed the worst. The office at Gareth Morgan Investments fielded hundreds of calls expressing condolences, and Newstalk ZB fielded 5500 calls from people asking whether it was us. Our families had a few anxious moments, although they were reassured by reports that both casualties were on one bike, whereas they knew we were riding our own machines. It took a little longer before those who knew our intended route and had been following our progress concluded that it couldn't have been us: we'd already passed through Turkey, and were readying ourselves to pass through the scene of a recent Uzbek uprising that Karimov had brutally suppressed.

After the enforced break in Tashkent, it was a relief to get on the road again. We rode east across Uzbekistan, reaching the Kyrgyzstan border via the spectacular Kamchik Pass and the beautiful Ferghana Valley. We were hoping to find a way of getting across the border that didn't involve entering Andijan, where 800 rioting civilians had been massacred by the army in Karimov's own version of Tiananmen Square. But we were turned back wherever we went, and so into Andijan it was. In the event, the only sign of the unrest we saw was a cordon of tanks stationed around the police checkpoint.

We had a relatively trouble-free crossing into Kyrgyzstan. Our first night was at Osh, in accommodation that was about as far from the centre of town as could be arranged. People were a bit jumpy about foreigners at that time, as Uzbeks had been fleeing across the border in large numbers to get away from the recent troubles. Gareth got talking to a young woman about the impending elections.

'You must be delighted to be living in the first country for miles to be having free elections,' he said.

She shook her head.

'It will be a disaster. There's already too much democracy in Kyrgyzstan,' she said gloomily.

'What?' said Gareth. 'You haven't even tried it yet.'

'Watch and wait,' she replied. 'We'll have the elections, someone will win, he'll ban all further elections and the loser will shoot him. Then we'll be right back where we started. We need the Soviets back, to keep order.'

Her prophesy proved only too mournfully accurate.

Gareth had to do a telephone interview with Paul Holmes that night. He had left the satellite phone with Dave, expecting to be able to use a landline from our accommodation. It turned out, however, that the hotel could only receive international calls, not make them. Gareth enlisted the help of the guide who was travelling in the van with the spouses, and learned that he would have to go to the exchange in the early hours to jack up the interview. A taxi was called, so he and Jo climbed into the battered old jalopy and set off for the exchange at one in the morning along a decrepit road in atrocious weather. Once there, the guide prevailed upon the operators to let Gareth phone Holmes. Against the odds, as it seemed, he got through, but as the on-air deadline was looming; they had another terrifying dash back to the hotel to arrive in time to field the incoming call from New Zealand. It all worked out: the show must go on.

We visited a silk works in the town. Silk, after all, was part of the reason we were here. We wondered what Marco Polo would have made of the machinery. It was a pretty impressive facility: Uzbekistan is the largest producer of silk in the world. It's all carefully government-controlled, with the state issuing silkworms to the industry at the beginning of each season and acting as sole marketing agent for the finished product.

We rode 280 km to Kara-Kul in the northwest of Kyrgyzstan, enjoying the scenery — soaring, snow-capped mountains, lush green alpine meadows — and the cooler temperatures. We got two bits of welcome news while we were there. First, we learned that the Chinese authorities had, for their own inscrutable reasons, put our entry to China back four days. And we got the other phone call we'd so desperately been awaiting: Dave called to say that the dead bike was back up, and they were on their way.

We moved on to beautiful Lake Issyk-Kul, the second highest navigable alpine lake in the world after Titicaca in Peru in which we'd swum just two years earlier. Issyk-Kul brought those memories flooding back and we checked into a motorcamp there determined to repeat the high-altitude swimming escapade. Bryan was pretty crook with a stomach complaint, so Jo put him to bed with a couple of tablets of codeine (or at least, she hoped that's what they were, given she'd bought them in Uzbekistan after carefully deciphering the Cyrillic script). Gareth was hardly much better off, and groaned most of the night, while Brendan and Jo cooked baked beans and sat toasting Russia and admiring the stars with the next-door neighbours — a Russian military officer and his wife who was the spitting image of Hot-Lips Houlihan from the TV series *M*A*S*H*. We couldn't stop staring at her.

The next day we took it easy. Brendan learned it was possible to go scuba diving in the lake, so he went off to do that. It was a pretty uninspiring dive, he reported, but still a thrill to think that, even on the lakebed, he was at a greater altitude than the summit of Mount Cook back home. Jo and Gareth, true to the spirit of these trips, took to the alpine waters in their togs, trying to be brave.

Meanwhile, back in Tashkent, Dave worked frantically to fit the newly arrived crankshaft transponder. Once he'd finished, he tried firing her up. There was a definite improvement — the bike would now start — but it wouldn't run. Mirmahdi (owner of Sanar Motors) and his team stepped in, and although their experience with bike electrics was limited (read: nonexistent), they were fairly sure they could find the fault. Dave and Selwyn rushed off to jack up emergency visas for Kazakhstan —a shortcut through that country on the expressway seemed likely to be the only way they would catch us up in time — and by the time they got back, a grinning Mirmahdi was sitting astride Selwyn's bike, gunning the sweetly throbbing motor. Barring disasters, it looked as though Sanar Motors had plucked Selwyn's Half Marco from the fire after all.

The next day, June 9, they hit the road for the big catch-up. The border crossing at Keles went smoothly, although there was some muttering among the massed officials about Dave's Uzbek visa, which had expired 24 hours previously. Then it was just a matter of riding as quickly as possible in the right direction. They crossed into Kyrgyzstan with no problems that evening, and stayed at the border town of Kara-Balta, distinguished, Dave was to relate, by providing the worst accommodation of the whole trip and no food. The following day, they decided they could allow themselves the luxury of a detour to Lake Issyk-Kul. They began to regret it as they approached the tollbooth on the road and were diverted into a lane of their own. The toll collector then demanded 500 Kyrgyz som (about NZ$15) per bike. Dave and Selwyn could see a tariff setting out tolls ranging from 40 to 500 som, and although they couldn't read the script alongside each amount, they figured the upper end of the range was more likely to apply to buses and trucks than to motorbikes. They sensed a 'tourist tax'. After some debate with a man who professed to speak no English, they grudgingly handed over 400 som apiece, just to get on their way.

They were still dark about it as they rode into the pretty town of Balykchy on the shores of the lake. Perhaps spleen affected their vision, because they both rode through a red traffic light. There was no traffic, so they survived what could have been a fatal mistake on another road in any other part of the world. But as Murphy's Law would have it, they did it right in front of a bored Kyrgyz traffic cop. They'd gone no more than 100 m when a large, white, Russian-made car overtook them with siren blaring. They pulled over obediently, and the uniformed officer of the unmarked car demanded to see all their documents — passports, bike registration papers and international driver's licences (the first time any of us were asked to produce these). Unlike the toll collector, the cop spoke enough English to deliver a lecture to the pair as they sat, chastened, in the back of his car, then demanded they hand over an instant fine of US$50. They expressed alarm and dismay at the amount and, between them, settled on US$10 each. The officer tut-tutted and shook his head, but took the money and drove off at a suspiciously jubilant clip. The miscreants were free to go. They had a swim in the lake to cool off, quietly satisfied at the 40 greenbacks they'd finessed from the Kyrgyz police force. They met up with the rest of us at Naryn about an hour later. Selwyn was hobbling a bit over the next few days from all the hard riding Dave had made him do, but at least we were all back together again.

The following day, the reconstituted Silk Rider sextet set out to visit the charity project we were sponsoring through our journey. Kyrgyzstan is a poor country yet to get on its feet since the collapse of the Soviet Union. It's small (the population is around 5 million) and remote, squeezed between Uzbekistan to the west and the behemoth, China, to the east. Its relationship with both has been prickly, as Kyrgyzstan has clung fiercely to its independence throughout its history.

Since the collapse of the USSR in the 1990s, all the former satellite states have suffered a dearth of foreign investment. While those with the luxury of revenue from oil and gas have been cushioned from the shock of transition, resource-poor Kyrgyzstan has felt the full impact. Its principal earner is the export to China of scrap metal from the derelict factories established there in the Soviet era and decommissioned at the time of the Soviet withdrawal. Needless to say, this is not a trade with long-term prospects.

The paucity of resources is, of course, reflected in state spending, and none is more poorly funded than the education sector. Annual funding per child is US$5 and falling. Compare that to the international median of US$2000 per annum and you can see how desperate is their need. For this reason — and precisely because, unlike the 'stans to the west, Kyrgyzstan at present is without a dictator following a bloodless coup, and with democratic elections scheduled to take place shortly after our visit — Kyrgyzstan appealed to us as the worthiest of the many worthy projects with which UNICEF is involved along our route.

In rural Kyrgyzstan, the traditional and still common lifestyle is nomadic. People live in yurts, so that they can up-pegs and move everything, people and livestock, to the *jailoo* (the alpine pastures) in the summer and back down to the valleys in winter. Those who have left this lifestyle behind are small-plot farmers with a few animals they watch over every day, and desultory plantings of crops. Their agricultural techniques are manual and therefore labour-intensive — machinery is rare — so Kyrgyz farms are worked by the whole family.

In this system children are a vital economic resource, and there's a natural tendency to work them all the time. Education is low on the average family's list of priorities, and this is what the UNICEF project is out to change. The idea has been to take a locality and mount an intensive effort not only to enrol children in schools, but also to ensure they attend. (Attendance is traditionally patchy: numbers fall away dramatically at harvest time, for example, and in winter, when the temperatures can drop as low as 50 degrees below zero). The expectation is that as the benefits of education are demonstrated among the target group, peer pressure will be mobilised on others to get a piece of it.

The UNICEF educational project — Community Management of Education — was inaugurated in 2004, and its achievements so far have been startling. The participation rate has lifted from 70 per cent in 2004 to 90 per cent today, although attendance is still part time for most, and 'invisible kids' — those whose existence was previously unknown — are constantly being discovered. Most of these are the little shepherds and goatherds who spend their days alone, high in the hills, tending the family's stock.

The project aims to involve the entire community in the education of their children — everyone from schoolteachers and principals to leaders of local government, social-welfare specialists, health-care professionals, law-enforcement agencies, local businesses, other non-governmental organisations and influential villagers. All participants are volunteers, motivated solely by their belief in the importance and value of education.

We visited a participant school in Alysh village, 30 minutes' ride from Naryn. On the way, we were carrying a young cameraman from Kyrgyz national television who had arrived that morning, positively reeking of vodka. Jo had foolishly said — a throwaway offer, which she never expected to be taken up — that he could ride pillion with her. But accept he did, with a little too much alacrity. It became pretty clear that the chance to hang onto Jo's waist was his real interest in the arrangement. We had to prise him off her and her bike. For some of the rest of the ride, he actually balanced on the back of Brendan's bike, standing and filming in the reverse direction to that in which the bike was travelling. It was impressive to witness, but his footage, when we got to watch it much later on, was all but unusable.

The UNICEF project operates at Alysh for half the year. All the children and their parents knew we were coming, and had been looking forward to our visit nearly as much as we had been. We observed the planning side of things — the rural education group mapped out the next academic year, based on the demands of agriculture and the exigencies of the seasons. Another group showed us a map of the village, which had a scheme of houses with the names of the students who lived in each on them. A sticker was affixed to the map alongside a student's name. A red sticker signified a student who was chronically absent, a yellow meant a student missed classes here and there and regular attendance earned a green sticker. This way, you could see an individual student's attendance record at a glance and quickly identify problems. There weren't a hell of a lot of green stickers to be seen.

That evening, we checked into our hotel and faced a barrage

of questions from the dozen or so Kyrgyz print and television journalists who descended on us. Interest was high: where, exactly, was New Zealand (the blow-up globe came in handy yet again), and what the hell were we doing in Kyrgyzstan? They were keen to hear our impressions of the countryside and of the people. When the journalists told Dave and Selwyn that the going rate of the spot fine for a local who has run a red light is US$1, their estimation of the Kyrgyz police went down. But we were able to be quite sincere as we told them we loved the country and were humbled by the welcome we had received.

We were able to turn all the media attention to our advantage, or at least to the advantage of the cause we were there to promote. Many of the journalists accompanied us the next day when we rode up to the remote village of At-Bashi, in the real Kyrgyz backblocks. We visited the bazaar, where you could see part of the reason school attendance is such a problem. There were kids everywhere, pushing barrows and manning stalls. They dropped everything when we arrived and crowded around us, staring at us and the bikes. Some of the bolder kids asked questions, and had their pictures taken on the bikes. One of them challenged Jo to a race. His best manly efforts were in vain — his sturdy Kyrgyz pony was no match for the flying BMW — but what a sight to behold.

After the bazaar, we visited a centre for disabled and disadvantaged children — and you know you're hard up when you're a disadvantaged kid in Kyrgyzstan. The centre is partly supported by a sewing workshop run by the women of the community. We bought a few bits and pieces and a beautifully worked, handmade carpet for 1000 som (about US$24). We also bought bottles of *kumys* — fermented mare's milk — from a roadside stall. Marco Polo had reported favourably that the taste of this drink was not unlike white wine. Who knows what Venetian white wine was like: we found *kumys* quite disgusting, like a tablet of Disprin in a glass of milk.

We then went to one of the local schools, which had only recently joined the UNICEF scheme. It was pretty primitive. The buildings had mud walls, an asbestos roof and rotten wooden floors. The classrooms had been designed to hold 12, but up to 30 were crammed in for any one lesson, as there were 300 on the roll, attending in shifts. You could see why school in winter is an unattractive prospect. Each room had a rough coal heater, but the local coal is poor quality and burns badly, filling the place with smoke. Most of the kids had respiratory problems as a direct result. There was no running water in the village, let alone in the school, and the toilets were longdrops set at a distance from the classroom block to minimise the stench. The supply of books was pathetic, there were certainly no computers to be seen, and the blackboards were installed during the Soviet era. There's no sports gear and nothing resembling laboratory equipment, of course, so science can be taught in theory only. It would have been depressing were it not for the dedication of the teachers and volunteers, and the sheer, irrepressible optimism of the kids.

The highlight of the visit for us was our discussion with the children themselves. We were able to talk to them in private, away from their parents and their teachers, and it was an interesting conversation. We asked what they liked and didn't like about school and their lives in general. We asked what they were aiming to do when they left school. Interestingly, given every single one of them came from a rural background, none of them wanted to be farmers. Their sights were set much higher: they wanted to be journalists, computer programmers, translators, policemen, fashion designers, writers — exactly what you'd expect a bunch of New Zealand kids to come out with. The difference, of course, is in the chances of a Kyrgyz kid living their dream compared with those of a New Zealander.

When we'd finished, we handed out books and picture cards and then gave the kids rides on the bikes. Their delight was infectious, and both sides learned in different ways about how it is possible to be moved. Dave was a particular hit, perhaps because he was so obviously a soft touch, and he practically had to use a crowbar to remove the last kids from his bike when the time came for us to go.

From At-Bashi, we headed to what passes for a resort in Kyrgyzstan, namely a cluster of yurts high up on the *jailoo* named Shepherd's Life. We were accompanied all the way by tiny kids on big horses, most of them riding bareback. The Kyrgyz have been horse-herders forever, and boy, can they ride. In the yurt, we were served a huge meal featuring the national dish, *shorpo* (a soup made from mutton — quite delicious), and, of course, more *kumys*. Someone warned us to go easy on the first courses, which comprised nuts and dried fruits, and we were grateful for the advice: we were each served the better part of a whole roast leg of lamb, and given a plastic bag for leftovers. We swapped yarns, told a few lies and sang a few songs — 'Pokarekare Ana', and 'Ten Guitars' — and the afternoon passed in splendid style.

Tackling the Taklamakan

June 13 was always going to be a big day. We had to cover some 300 km, at the outer limits of a comfortable day's ride for this type of terrain, and included in the itinerary was the 3572 m Torugart Pass. We woke to heavy rain, which was hardly promising. To add to it all, we had a deadline. We had to be at the Chinese border by 5 pm or we would miss our chance to enter. If that happened, unless we could sweet-talk the notoriously intransigent Chinese authorities, the trip would to all intents and purposes end there.

We set off after our usual breakfast and reading from Marco. For the first hour or so, slithering in mud and deep gravel, passing the yawing articulated trucks belching black smoke, carrying loads of scrap metal from the dismantled Soviet factories of Kyrgyzstan to the foundries of China, we were all imagining the various things that could go wrong. Bryan was knackered, having suffered from the debilitating Silk Road squirts for longer than the rest of us. Bryan's bike was all but knackered, too, the slack chain slipping from time to time and making an awful noise. Dave had done what he could to tighten it, but we all knew it was going to go sooner or later.

Sure enough, after a couple of hours the dramas commenced. The front bikes noticed the unsettling absence of headlights in their mirrors. They waited, then turned and headed back. A little way back, we found Brendan putting the finishing touches to a puncture repair. It wasn't long before Dave, who by now was pretty consistently taking up the rear, came along. As soon as Brendan was back up, we were off.

We had planned to make a detour to Tash Rabat, the site of the tenth-century caravanserai at which Marco Polo had stopped over. We were pretty keen to get there, but it involved crossing a river, and Bryan didn't like the look of it. He'd begun the day pretty tired.

'Nope,' he said. 'I'm not doing it. You lot go if you want to, but I'm waiting here. No way you're getting me in that.'

Jo was inclined to think he was right. It was a cold day, and the water was colder still. If someone fell, they would be in real strife getting the bike back and getting warm again. Perhaps it wasn't worth the risk.

Cometh the hour, cometh the man; in this case, Dave.

'What the hell's the hold-up?' he yelled.

Jo explained their misgivings to him. Bryan reaffirmed his intention to stay put. Dave coaxed disgusted noises from the engine of his bike and rode through the stream without further ado. Bryan and Jo watched the water rising up to his lap and didn't feel a hell of a lot better.

On the other bank he waited, hands on hips, as the rest of us debated it.

'Come on, woman!' he yelled. When that got no response, he kicked his bike back onto its stand and commenced wading into the river.

'I'll come and take your bike over for you girl!' he roared.

Jo reluctantly headed into the river, kicking the bike into second so that she had power available if she hit something in midstream. The idea is to pick your line and stick to it, trying to keep a steady speed. After all, the one thing you must not do on a river crossing is stop, because then you're over and off. You tend to keep the revs up and control your progress with the clutch, hoping that if you hit a big obstruction of any sort, you'll either ride up and over it or slide off the sides. At all costs, though, just keep going.

She got across. The water was intensely cold, and it soaked not only her trousers but also the sheepskin on her saddle and everything she carried in her panniers.

The caravanserai was an awesome destination, however. There it sat at the end of a long valley wedged into the side of the hillside, just as it had ten centuries earlier. Eagles soared high above its stone walls and we felt very remote arriving at this travellers' inn so far from anywhere. Inside, we wandered room to room stepping around the mounds of ice that had yet to thaw from the floors. Summer up here is all too short. To think Marco was here within these walls. It was pretty special.

Back out to the main road we rejoined Bryan and wound our way up into the mountains, the temperature dropping, the weather remaining foul. Another puncture. This time it was Dave's bike, and again, the rider had it well in hand by the time we got back to see what was up. No sooner had Dave got his fixed than someone else got a flat. By now, it was seriously cold — down to 3 degrees Celsius, by the thermometers we were carrying — so standing around waiting for the repairs to be effected was not much fun. We were queuing up for a turn on the foot-pump, a job not many of us relished under ordinary circumstances. Our case wasn't helped by the trucks which bounced and crashed past, emptying the muddy contents of potholes all over us. Watching bits of iron and rubbish bouncing along in their wake, we pretty quickly established why it was that after nearly 10,000 km puncture-free, we'd had three in a heap today. Once we were up and running again, we occasionally saw a truck off the side of the road. We'd cheer. It's funny how quickly the road can turn you into a mean son of a bitch.

We got up and over the Torugart Pass without further incident, although we were all suffering the effects of altitude to greater or lesser degrees, and our bikes were struggling with the combination of lean mixtures due to the thin air and the low-octane fuel. The downhill leg was like a mudslide.

Just into the descent and we were all wet, covered in mud and bloody cold by the time we reached the first of the Chinese border gates, 120 km uphill from our drop-dead destination, the Customs processing facility at the bottom of the Tien Shan Range. Here, we met the guide prearranged to accompany us through the border formalities and into China. He was a short bloke, with wire-framed glasses and a pretty engaging manner. His Chinese name was unpronounceable. We knew another group had hired the same fellow, but we couldn't remember the European name they'd used. We asked if Rick would do. It would, he reckoned. We learned later the previous group had called him John, or something like that. He who pays the piper, and all that. 'Rick' introduced us to his driver, who was to be accompanying us in a van. Then we set off again.

Time was slipping away, and the deadline for making the Chinese Customs point was looming. We lost a bit when we were held up by a queue of traffic, stopped behind an overturned truck that was blocking the road up ahead. We decided we had to go off-road to get around the obstruction, and so we got Rick out of his Land Cruiser, into some more or less suitable clothes — less a helmet — stuck him on the back of Brendan's bike and sent them packing as fast as possible for the Customs point.

We hadn't got too much further when Gareth, who was riding second, noticed that there was no sign of Selwyn behind him. He stopped. Then Bryan appeared, looking haggard. Gareth waved him through. That was two bikes in front, three behind somewhere. After ten minutes or so of riding back he came across Selwyn, who seemed confused. He had gone back, he said, but after riding for a while

Above: *Ashgabat, Turkmenistan — the Las Vegas of the Karakum, complete with gold domes and fountains.*

Below: *A fishing boat high and dry at Moynaq, Uzbekistan. The former Soviet regime's irrigation projects worked — but prevented water getting down to the Aral Sea.*

Above: *'Fairydown City' in the Karakum.*

Below: *Khiva, an ancient Mongol fortress.*

Above: *One of ours amidst the locals in Bukhara town square, Uzbekistan.*

Below: *An old-timer ready to leave with us in Kochkor, Kyrgyzstan.*

Above: *Sermon on the mount — a Kyrgyz mosque.*

Left: *Dave and Brendan deal with yet another puncture repair in Torugart Pass, racing against the clock to enter China.*

Above: *UNICEF educational project in Kyrgyzstan.*

Below: *Pony is the preferred mode of transport in At-Bashi, Kyrgyzstan.*

Above: *Dave sits a healthy distance away from one of the Taklamakan Desert twisters.*

Below: *A Chinese Turkestani girl fetches our lunch dumplings out of a steamer.*

Above: *Exhausted Silkies after a day of sandstorms and suffocating heat.*

Below: *Outdoor pool in China.*

Right: *First glimpse of the Great Wall — a beacon tower in the middle of the Taklamakan Desert.*

Below: *Journey's end — the Silk Riders near the eastern end of the Great Wall, Beijing.*

without seeing anyone, he'd begun to think he'd missed everyone and was now last. He'd turned around and headed towards China again. He had no idea where Jo or Dave, tail-end Charlie, were. Poor old Selwyn: the altitude had clearly got to him.

Over half an hour had elapsed since the riding order had first been disrupted. Gareth kept heading back toward Kyrgyzstan in search of Jo and Dave. Jo had already turned back, contemplating Dave lying under a bike in the cold. While she took some comfort knowing it was good old bulletproof Dave back there, nevertheless she was relieved when, after ten minutes of backtracking, she saw him beside his bike, clearly intact and attending to something mechanical.

Dave looked up as she approached, and she saw his shoulders droop.

'Christ, Jo. Why'd it have to be you?' he said as she pulled up.

'Charming,' she replied.

'Well, you haven't got any bloody tubes, have you?'

This was true. Jo had the medical kit, and would have been the ideal person to arrive on the scene had this been an injury situation. But for Dave, pissed off at getting his second puncture of the day — and the fourth the group had suffered, every one of them a rear wheel, so much harder to fix than the front — a rescue party comprising the only Silk Rider who wasn't carrying puncture gear was a less than welcome sight.

'How long until someone else comes back?' Dave wanted to know.

'About an hour,' Jo replied.

'Hell,' Dave winced. 'We'll never make the bloody border. We'll have to bodgie something up.'

While they were engaged in pulling the rear brakes and the gear cluster apart to get the wheel off, a battered bike pulled up and a mongrel-looking pair of local yokels got off. If their intention was to help, they had a funny way of going about it. One of them began fossicking through the tools that Dave had laid out, while the other one grabbed Jo's upper arm hard to restrain her and enough to hurt her and (as we later observed) bruise her. Dave had to abandon his attempts to fix the tyre and warn them off, brandishing the biggest spanner he was packing. Between them, Dave and Jo made what progress they could to patch the already patched-up tube with parcel tape and glue, all the while keeping an eye on their hovering attendants.

Time and patience was running out all round. When Gareth arrived with Selwyn in tow, finding Dave and Jo fighting off a pair of individuals who looked like they were straight out of a Chinese remake of *Deliverance*, he waded straight in. Hell hath no fury like an economist watching his carefully planned and costed expedition being derailed through delays, and he carried the day. The miscreants were persuaded to get back on their bike and piss off. The repair, such as it was, was carried out in comparative peace. With no time to lose, and little faith in their handiwork, they got going again.

The tyre was gradually deflating all the way down the rest of the mountain pass, but somehow they made it to the Customs post. Ironically, the officials discovered a problem with Dave's paperwork, and although we were admitted to China, his bike was locked up overnight while it was sorted anyway.

Apart from that, the only further mishap on this long, hard day came when Gareth was being waved over to the side by a border guard. The rain had glazed the tiles of the forecourt, and he slithered over, muffled curses accompanying the righting of his bike.

Still, here we were in China, and two things struck us at once. The food and the beer were exquisite. After the long, long, frustrating day, we cleaned ourselves up, settled into our hotel and enjoyed both. Kashgar (or Kashi, as it is known these days), the town in which we were staying, was pretty cool. Look out one window of the hotel and you could see the mountains over which we'd just come. Look out the other and you could see the Taklamakan Desert, which we were about to cross.

Kashgar was a crossroads on the silk routes of the ancient world, linking China to Europe in the west via Samarkand and Constantinople, and India and Pakistan in the south, via the Karakoram Range and over the Pamirs. It's the biggest city in Xinjiang (or Chinese Turkestan, as it sometimes gets called) which, at one sixth the total size of China (four times the total land area of New Zealand), and with a population of 19 million, is the largest province in China. Actually it's not a province at all: it's one of the country's so-called 'autonomous regions', along with Tibet and Inner Mongolia. It's difficult to understand what exactly is autonomous about these areas, where ethnic minorities once dominated. They remain answerable to Beijing in all respects. In common with the others, Xinjiang has endured its fair share of 'ethnic swamping', as millions of Han (ethnic) Chinese have been sent here to alter the ethnic mix. Until the early 1990s, the overwhelmingly dominant ethnicity hereabouts was the Uyghurs who, like the Kazakhs and the Kyrgyzs, are one strand of the Turkic nomads who historically populated Central Asia. Since then, however, and as a result of the deliberate demographic engineering of Beijing, they have declined from an 80 per cent majority to be 50/50 with the Han.

The tensions are obvious. The Uyghurs to whom we spoke told us how much they hated being ruled by the Han, and assured us there would be secession at some stage. Yet from what we could gather, the Uyghur claims to the region aren't as clear cut as they would have you believe. Intermittent Han Chinese control of this region can be traced as far back as AD 73, and it was a Buddhist stronghold before Islam got a grip in AD 1400. And while there are tensions, the lid is more or less kept on them by prosperity. The reason Beijing bothers with this remote region at all is the abundance of natural resources to be found there. Apparently, there's more oil and gas beneath Xinjiang than beneath the entire United States, and Beijing has thrown money at the infrastructure to assist in its exploitation. The region's economic output has been growing by 10 per cent since the 1990s, and some of this wealth has evidently trickled down to the population to ease the pangs of nationalist misgiving.

Speaking of trickling down, Rick approached Gareth upon our arrival in Kashgar and told him that he needed to come and meet the van driver, who was finishing up there and wanted to say goodbye. Reading between the lines, Gareth spotted the expectation that the driver would also receive a tip for services rendered. He swiftly disabused Rick of this notion. We had specifically told Murray and Pat of Silk Road Adventures that we didn't want to get into tipping situations in any of the countries where we were travelling, and that if tipping were part of the setup, it should be built into our bill. Gareth told Rick that his tips were in the hands of his employers. Rick didn't seem too impressed by this, but he didn't argue.

After the previous day's epic, the bikes were all gunged up with mud and needed high-pressure hosing as badly as we had upon arrival. Gareth refused to do his. He had a radio interview to do, he said, and he had to upload the latest batch of photos to the Silk Rider website. No one so much as murmured: this was the way the division of labour was working by now, and it was working very well.

We had originally planned to have a few days' rest in Kashgar, although that plan was made to allow for the very real possibility that we would lose time somewhere in the lead-up. As it was, we had just the two nights there. We endured our day off, spending it at the car wash getting the clothes and bikes washed of their mountain mud.

Next day, June 14, Rick's new driver joined us. 'Jim' was a storybook Chinaman to look at, nattily dressed with long, Fu Manchu facial hair. We all liked him a lot. We saddled up and, with Rick riding in Jim's Toyota Land Cruiser, headed into the fearsome Taklamakan Desert, the world's second largest. In Marco's day, people attached to the Taklamakan the cheerful slogan: 'if you go in, you won't come out.' To the east, the Chinese took this literally, using it as a penal option by banishing miscreants outside the limits of China as delineated by the Great Wall, confident that either the desert or the Mongol hordes would serve the purposes of justice. Bearing all this in mind, the crossing was not something we took lightly, but like Marco himself, cross it we must if we were to get to our journey's end.

At first, to our astonishment, we were travelling on an amazing road, namely the Tarim Highway, which crosses this vast desert 522 km from south to north. The Taklamakan has literally swallowed cities in its restlessly shifting sands. The job of keeping this vast, beautiful highway from suffering the same fate is enormous and is accomplished by caretakers who man water wells every 3 km along the route. The water is used to irrigate vegetation planted on each side which, along with acres of matting woven from flax, is intended to stabilise the sand and hold back the desert. And any stray grains that get by are swept off the carriageway with hand-brooms. It's a typically Chinese way of doing things: labour, after all, is hardly a scarce resource in a country of nearly two billion people.

The highway was fine until the authorities started turfing us off on the grounds that motorbikes were 'agricultural machinery'. And after a couple of days' riding, we were out in the desert proper, the sand and scrubby vegetation giving way to shingle and finally to great, soaring dunes alternating with achingly wide salt pans. At the height of the day, the heat made these expanses of salt shimmer blue in the distance, so there were times when we could have sworn we were heading toward great lakes, perhaps even in sight of the far edge of the desert, days ahead of schedule. We had been told that the temperature regularly nudges 70 degrees Celsius out here, helped by lack of shade and radiation from the sandy terrain. We weren't there in the hottest part of the year, but it still effortlessly reached 47 degrees Celsius. That was plenty hot enough for us.

The landforms were stunning, a photographer's paradise. At one of our overnight camping stops, Jo took off into the dunes with her bright red silk sleeping-bag liner, into which she climbed to roll down the hill while our shutters clattered.

At times we were 400 km from the nearest settlement: that's how remote this part of the world is. We camped out on a couple of the six nights it took us to cross the desert. The fey wind which haunts the Taklamakan kept us awake, flogging the tents erratically all night, and half-burying the bikes in sand. It was an extraordinary place to be. The other nights we stayed in little oasis villages, the centre of the usual avid attention. At one of these stops, Jo got out her medical kit to attend to a sore finger one of the boys had acquired. In no time flat, a queue of locals had formed behind him to receive some of the 'witch-doctor's' attentions.

As you get further away from Kashgar and the population thins out, you begin to see the family resemblance between the traditional Uyghur way of life and that of their Turkic cousins of the rest of Central Asia. Chinese-style housing disappears, replaced by mud huts, and motor vehicles are supplanted by donkey-carts. As in many of the other remote parts of the world we have visited, we were amazed by the dogged human capacity to eke out a living anywhere. You'd be in the middle of the desert, a couple of hundred kilometres from the last town, a hundred more before the next, and there would be some bloke with his donkey, or an old truck from which someone was selling melons.

We were doing big days, because after the five-day delay at the China border we were anxious to catch up with our schedule in order to keep some of the appointments we had made further down the line. One day saw us cover over 300 km on gravel, sand and rocks, including up and over a 4000 m pass, which had the bikes struggling on their low-octane fuel and their riders struggling on the low-octane air. Strangely for the middle of a desert, there was a river in the mountains. Jo had a dip in the chocolate-brown water, which was surprisingly cool. We managed to persuade a tollgate attendant to let our bikes onto the highway for the last 80 km. After the rough tracks we'd been using for the last four days, gliding along on the beautiful asphalt surface was like flying.

Somewhere along the way, our resident tight-arses, Dave and Jo, confided their suspicions of Rick, who had assumed control of all our negotiations and dealings with hotels, restaurants and the like. They were pretty sure he was adding a slice for himself and Jim into the price he passed on to us, perhaps as an underhand way of recovering the tips he considered he was missing out on. You can ignore a little bit of graft, but only up to a point. And besides, for both Dave and Jo, half the fun of travelling is dealing with the locals over such things as accommodation and meals. They saw no reason to forgo this pleasure, particularly if they were going to have to pay for the privilege. Wherever possible, they insisted on making our arrangements themselves. Once again, Rick didn't argue, but he began to claim that he didn't know towns we were approaching and politely directed us to stay on the outskirts while he scouted ahead. These 'scouting' missions usually involved setting up our meals and accommodation. For the rest of us, this battle of wills was a fascinating spectacle.

We had one thrilling encounter with the Marco Polo story around here. In the middle of the desert, which is to say, in the middle of nowhere, we came across a huge complex — a factory or a mine or some such, we couldn't quite tell. Piled high around it were great heaps of a white substance, which from a distance looked like snow. White dust whirled in the air, too. It was while reading from Marco about his own observations in this area, where he mentions the curiosity of a white rock called 'salamander', which could be mined, crumbled into fibres and woven into a cloth that couldn't be burned, that we realised what we were seeing: asbestos mining. Given the bad name it has in public-health circles back home, we hoped the dust we were riding through and breathing was the benign form of asbestos. But we were also blown away by the connection with Marco's own story: we were seeing the modern operation exploiting a resource that he had seen mined himself, in precisely the same spot. It is details like this that, for us, put to rest any doubt that Marco Polo actually made the journey he said he had made.

We created a real stir in the little town, Mangnai, in which we ended that day. We were, the locals told us, the first big-noses to visit in two years. People crowded around us, and followed us wherever we went. We had worked up a powerful thirst in the course of the long, hard day. We found a beer 'garden', which consisted of a concrete yard surrounded by derelict buildings. No matter: we were there for the beer, not the garden. The beer in China is wonderful, if only more of it was chilled — in those temperatures we hung out for *bing piju* (cold beer). Afterward we climbed, all six of us, into an old lady's taxi and went to an internet café. Later, we had a huge, delicious meal for the equivalent of NZ$1 apiece.

One of the by-products of the intense heat in the desert is the sandstorms for which the Taklamakan is famous. Many of these take the form of little twisters that look very similar to miniature tornadoes — for the very good reason that this is what they are — and sometimes these streaked the skyline like prison bars. As many as 20 could be clearly visible on each side of the track at any one time.

For the first few days, we played Russian roulette with them. Occasionally we'd be buffeted by sudden, strong winds, and most of the time we were riding in a wind-borne haze of sand that made it feel as though you had sandpaper between your teeth. But we hadn't tangled with any of the really nasty storms. Some roared across the track ahead of us, some passed behind the bikes.

Eventually, of course, some law of statistics decreed our luck would run out. On our second-to-last day in the Taklamakan, we were tootling along when we noticed a dramatic plunge in temperature accompanied by heavy rain.

Great, thought Bryan. That'll keep the bloody dust and sand down.

That, it turned out, was generally true of the dust and sand, but suddenly, just ahead and to his left, Bryan saw a particularly rapidly moving twister picking up the sand and mud, wet or not, and whirling it around madly as it steered a collision course with him. He realised that at his current speed, he would intersect with it just as it crossed the road, so he braked. It passed across the track some 20 m ahead.

Whew, he thought. That was close.

Seconds later, however, an even more menacing-looking funnel appeared to his left, apparently lining him right up. He had to make a quick decision: stop the bike and risk being blown, bike and all, off the road and down the steep bank to the side, or accelerate and get the bike stable enough to take a very strong side-blast of wind, rain and sand?

Bryan chose the latter, moving to the centre of the road just in time to be engulfed by the tornado. He realised quickly that he had badly underestimated the ferocity of the winds. He later reckoned the wind-speed to be well over 80 km/h, and he's probably right: the wind-speeds in the least powerful of American tornadoes routinely reach almost twice that. The visibility was suddenly nil. It was all he could do to make out his front wheel. His track veered to the right and he found himself at the edge of the road. With his full-face helmet full of wet sand and dust and his eyes stinging, he was, as he later put it, 'in praying mode'. He opened the throttle and steered to where he guessed the centre of the road to be and then, suddenly, he was out the other side of the maelstrom. He couldn't say afterward how long he was in the twister. It could have been ten seconds, or even less. It felt like ten minutes. He pulled over to the side of the road and seconds later Selwyn pulled up alongside. He had received a bit of a cuff from the funnel as well. They compared notes, and both agreed they had been very lucky not to have been blown off the road and down the bank.

A short time later Dave pulled up, roaring with laughter, and took a photo of what looked for all the world like a statue of a Silkie on his bike rendered from the mud and sand of the Taklamakan.

Six days and 2600 km after we entered China, we finally reached Dunhuang, on the western perimeter of the Taklamakan. Here, we could consider ourselves to be entering China proper, where the population density begins to lift to levels we stereotypically associate with this most populous of all nations, and where the composition of the population becomes virtually exclusively Han Chinese. The Taklamakan had been an unforgettable adventure, one of the highlights of the trip. But after all that sand, we were pretty ready to rest our eyes on something green. For the time being, beer bottles had to do.

Up the wall

Just before we exited the Taklamakan, Bryan, Brendan and Dave finally got around to fitting the new solenoid for Gareth's push-button start system which Dave had been carrying since Tashkent. By now, of course, Gareth had just about got used to the elaborate ritual required to use the Volga System that Dave and Bryan had jury-rigged. This was a good thing, because the new solenoid failed after only a day of operation. Dave and Bryan refitted the trusty Volga unit, which meant that the Chinese, like the populations of countries further west, were treated to the spectacle of Gareth fiddling with the toggle between his legs to start his bike, with the occasional memory lapse causing starting glitches and losses of control to cap off the entertainment.

Something was clearly overloading the solenoid on his bike, and the most plausible theory seemed to be that it was a problem with the wiring loom causing a short circuit and a voltage drop. Selwyn's bike — the one he had taken over from Phil — had suffered from just such a problem in Uzbekistan.

Our other chief mechanical concern was the ongoing sloppiness of the chain on Bryan's bike. But apart from punctures and the rear mud-deflectors — little plastic flaps suspended almost as an afterthought below the rear mudguards to comply with some German standard or another — which had self-dismantled on every bike in the Balkans as soon as the going got tough, that was the sum total of our technical problems. Not bad considering we'd already travelled more than 15,000 km over extremely variable terrain.

Dunhuang is situated on the southern fringe of the Lop Nor Desert, of which Marco Polo wrote, 'a marvellous thing was related . . . when travellers are on the move by night, and one of them chances to lag behind or to fall asleep or the like, when he tries to gain his company again he will hear spirits talking, and will suppose them to be his comrades. Sometimes the spirits will call him by name; and thus shall a traveller often-times be led astray so that he never finds his party. And in this way many have perished.' We didn't get to try our own luck with the voluble spirits, however, as Lop Nor these days is a centre of the Chinese nuclear-testing programme.

During our day off in Dunhuang, most of us went to see the famous Mogao Grottoes, or the Caves of 1000 Buddhas, an amazing structure carved into a rocky cliff-face at the edge of the desert. It all began in AD 366 when a Buddhist monk carved one Buddha figure into the rock. Over the next 1500 years, others added to it, the carvings depicting not only Buddha — although, as the name suggests, there are plenty of Buddhas — but also the life of the local people. In the early 20th century, a chamber was discovered off the main tunnels containing thousands of manuscripts that had been sealed up in the 11th century. Explorers from England, Germany, Russia and other places — real-life Raiders of the Lost Ark — pillaged the place to such an extent that most of its artefacts are now dispersed about museums worldwide. This is a mixed blessing, as museums in wealthier countries do preservation work much better than the

Chinese have been capable of doing. But it's a yawning absence in the cultural life of China, which is striving to acquire an artistic and cultural significance to rival its status in other global forums. Even in their reduced state, the caves were an awesome sight, a reminder of the antiquity of Chinese civilisation.

Gareth, meanwhile, spent the day from eight in the morning to eight at night in a crowded, smoky internet café uploading pictures to the website. We had managed this smoothly enough throughout the trip, but perhaps because of heavy Chinese usage of the available infrastructure, it was painfully slow in China. It would sometimes take as long as 30 minutes to upload a single low-resolution picture. The website may have been a popular and valuable resource, but there were times — such as at Dunhuang — where it became a millstone around our necks.

Just north of Dunhuang, once we set off again on June 22, we shortly came to one of the great landmarks of our journey. Rearing up from the sand was a lone beacon tower, about 20 m high, the westernmost end of the chain of beacon towers that, with their connecting ramparts, comprise the Great Wall of China. A few more kilometres down the track, we saw more evidence — more towers, and then continuous sections of the wall itself. It's not until you get close that you can fully appreciate the size of the wall and the unimaginable feat of engineering it was to build these massive structures.

The Great Wall is actually several walls, built at different stages and in different styles over a period of 1500 years from around 500 BC, and from whatever materials were most readily to hand. At this western end, the wall was actually a rammed-earth double wall with a deep ditch within it. The massive stone wall with which most people are familiar from tourist photographs and postcards begins much farther east. The beacon towers, however, were pretty similar the length of the wall, so far as we could tell. These were spaced at regular intervals providing line-of-sight communication from one end of the series of walls to the other. If a section of the line were attacked, a fire would be lit atop the nearest tower. Seeing this, the next tower along would light a signal fire and so on, down the line. Troops would hurry to reinforce the point where the original fire was kindled. It is said, and perhaps it's true, that word of an attack on the westernmost tower would reach the easternmost, 10,000 km distant, in less than 30 minutes.

It was intensely moving to see that first tower. It marked our arrival in China proper, and the beginning of the end of our long, long journey. We wondered how Marco must have felt upon arriving at the same point, after his ordeal in the Taklamakan.

We stopped for a while at Jiuyuguan, the point where the ancient Silk Road passed through the wall and headed south down the Hexi Corridor toward its eastern terminus in the old Chinese capital of Xian. The museum at Jiuyuguan has a lot of absorbing displays on the Wall. We learned that all of the walls are oriented west to east, as they were intended to protect the peaceable, pastoralist Chinese from the warrior 'nomad hordes' of the north. In all, an incredible 25,000 km of walls were constructed, manned at the height of China's defensive powers by a million warriors at any one time. And we learned that for all the grandeur of the vision and the unspeakable tenacity of its execution, it was probably the greatest folly in human history. Genghis Khan, leader of the aforementioned nomadic hordes, simply used the mobility his horses gave him to outflank the line, in the same way the Germans strolled past the Maginot Line during the Second World War. The fortress at Jiuyuguan, which has been fully restored, is a stunning sight against the backdrop of the pleated, snow-capped Qilian Mountains. The breathtaking Hexi Corridor, the narrow, fertile valley at the foot of the Qilian range, was to be our route for the next 100 km.

One thing we noticed in China as opposed to the Islamic countries through which we'd lately passed was the absence of the extreme reticence about matters sexual. As in places such as Turkey or Iran, everyone in China was fascinated by the appearance of a group comprising one woman and five men. But whereas in the benighted countries to the west they simply assumed the worst, the Chinese were merely unashamedly curious. Through sign language, women regularly asked Jo whom she was with out of the five boys, and gave no indication of being about to judge her no matter what combination she came up with. The Chinese men assumed she was 'with' them all.

In one village, Dave found himself on the receiving end of the same kind of prurient attention. He's a big fella, Dave, even the Dave-Lite he'd become through routine Silk Road weight loss. His stature intrigued the diminutive Chinese, women and men, and clearly set them to making wild anatomical extrapolations. At the village in question, Dave became aware of the calculating stares of a group of men who, when he looked at them enquiringly, began making fairly unambiguous gestures in their groin region and raising their eyebrows interrogatively. With a poker face, Dave held up his hands with the palms an improbable distance apart. On the other side of the ethnological and linguistic divide, jaws dropped. Suddenly, their hands were full of cash. Plainly, they were having a whip-round so that they could see the mythological proportions of the Tauranga cocky's private member. We decided it was time to go, for whatever Dave might try to tell you, here was a whole village full of people doomed to disappointment.

One of the scheduled stops we had set up from New Zealand was a visit to Shandan Bailie School, a modern, state-run equivalent to our polytechnics, currently undertaking the vocational training of 1500 students. Shandan Bailie, improbably as it seems when you roll in from the desert, is a sister school to Darfield College in Canterbury, and it is also one of the educational institutions founded by New Zealander Rewi Alley.

Alley came to China from New Zealand in 1927, and landed in Shanghai, where he observed a society ravaged by the worst excesses of the unfettered capitalism practised by the Kuomintang, the Chinese nationalist regime. Partly as a reaction to what he saw there, Alley embraced communism, and established a system of vocational training and workers' co-operatives among the Chinese peasantry. His intention was to protect them from domination, whether by their own people or by foreigners, through developing their skills to a level where their communities were perfectly self-reliant.

In 1943 he moved his vocational school and network of Gung Ho (literally 'work together') co-operatives to Shandan in the northwest corner of the Hexi Corridor, beyond the reach of the invading Japanese. Safely established there, his co-operatives provided production support for the battalions resisting the Japanese and thereafter the communists in their civil war against the Kuomintang.

It was fascinating to compare the transformation of China that Alley witnessed in the late 1940s — from unfettered capitalism to communism — with the almost diametrically opposed transition it is undergoing today, from communism to a socialist market economy.

There's no doubt the policies of liberalisation have been responsible for a quantum leap in the general living standards of the population. The Chinese have had a reputation throughout history as natural capitalists, the world's greatest entrepreneurs, and they have wasted little time in grasping the free-market nettle. New and growing businesses abound. The adjustment of the political system is lagging behind the economic transformation: it remains, of course, a one-party system, with debate stifled and any whiff of dissent ruthlessly suppressed, as with the massacre in Beijing's Tiananmen Square in 1989.

But it has to be recognised that communism is not the dirty word in China that it is elsewhere in the world. The depredations of the Kuomintang and the marauding Japanese are comparatively recent — the parents of today's Chinese teenagers remember well the brutality and hardship, and recall that it was communism that rescued the Chinese people from starvation and restored their national prestige. Communism has not failed in China in the way in which it so abjectly did in the USSR. The process of change is more likely to be slow, indexed to the rising standard of living afforded by the booming economy, than to occur by revolution.

For his part in the rescue of the peasantry, Rewi Alley is revered. We were treated like royalty simply by virtue of the fact we were from Alley's homeland. Mr Chen, the principal of Shandan Bailie School, welcomed us and we were given a reception of almost civic proportions by the students. We were only too pleased to give the students who had topped their classes in their recent exams rides on the bikes as rewards. It was a wonderful intercultural experience. Jill Spicer from Palmerston North, the sole foreigner in town and a teacher at Shandan Bailie, was a delightful host and Jo and she couldn't stop chatting.

The worst aspect of covering this section of the trip, the southern fringe of the Gobi Desert, was that we were forced to do it more or less off-road. There is a beautiful highway traversing the southern margin of the desert, but because our bikes were classed as 'farm machinery', we were not entitled to use it. We were relegated instead to the network of gravel and sand tracks that run alongside it. So you'd be struggling along on bumpy, soft, treacherous surfaces, eating the dust of other vehicles, sharing it with everything from donkey-carts and bicycles to farm trucks and tractors, and livestock ranging from pigs and cattle to people, while the superhighway right alongside you, close enough for you to touch the safety barrier, was empty apart from the occasional passing truck. It caused a few foul-ups in our riding order. You'd come across a line of traffic, and perhaps the lead bike would go along the outside while some or all of the following bikes would go along the inside. By the time you all missed one another, there was no way of knowing who was ahead or who was behind. Tempers flared somewhat in the heat. We had several goes at getting our bikes onto the highway, but we were waved off again by officials every time.

So off-piste — and pissed off — we remained. On one particularly bad stretch, which consisted of about a hundred miles of roadworks, Jo came to grief. She was just plunging into the deep sand on a steep off-ramp that had been constructed to avoid culverting work — conservatively, the fiftieth such obstruction we had negotiated that day — when a big black dog rushed her. She found herself face down in the dust beside her still-running bike, braced for the sensation of canines sinking into her flesh. Some of the roadworkers, who had seen what happened, chased the dog away, but Jo's leg was at a strange angle to her body with the bike on top of it. Dave, who had also witnessed the spill from a way back, raced up and stopped. He muttered that the leg didn't look good as he killed the bike and lifted it off her. After sitting there for a bit, gingerly flexing it, Jo declared her leg to be fine. She was, Dave agreed with her, lucky she was such a 'frexable' lady.

Nevertheless, it was easily another hundred kilometres of gravel and sand before we all stopped for lunch, whereupon Jo declined to eat anything and simply went to sleep. She was sore all over — the leg, of course, but also her ribs, which continued to trouble her for a few days afterward — and the Captain, in his role as deputy medic, declared her to be suffering from 'delayed shock'.

After we'd reached our stop for the night and she had self-administered a few restorative beers, Jo was fine, as she was quick to tell everyone, so long as she didn't breathe.

The next morning, some of the strain of the long days in difficult terrain began to tell. At breakfast, Gareth raised the subject of the poor mileages we'd been covering over the last few days, and how late we were getting where we needed to go. It was like taking the cork out of a bottle of shaken-up fizzy drink: everyone had been feeling the frustration, and everyone had a theory. Gareth listened for a bit, only really taking exception when Brendan ventured that it was all because individuals weren't riding fast enough.

No way, Gareth reckoned. There was another problem, and it had to be sorted out. The reason we were so slow across the ground was simple. We weren't sticking with the rider etiquette that had served us so well since leaving Munich all those weeks ago. Stress, fatigue, whatever the reason — those out front were losing touch with the bike immediately behind them. There began the collapse of group-riding etiquette. Anyone can ride fast, but if they don't stay in touch it forces others to cover for them, and the whole group gets slowed down. We set out that morning pretty tense.

It didn't help that along the road to Langzhou, we had a problem with Rick. At one point, when we'd lost a rider, the guide had insisted he had gone through and was ahead of us. Jo disagreed. Taking her word for it rather than Rick's, Gareth went back. Sure enough, there was Dave beside his bike, examining the wiring loom. An oil light had come on, and he was trying to work out whether it signified a lubrication problem or yet another electrical niggle. Gareth rather lost faith in Rick at this point.

When we had set off for Langzhou that morning, Rick showed Gareth on the map which roads they were going to take, and at which forks confusion was likely to arise. He neglected to do the same for the others. Gareth had passed through an intersection, acting on the guide's instructions and assuming everyone else would do the same, when he realised he had no one behind him. They, of course, were observing the etiquette: if you arrived at an intersection and were uncertain of the way you should take, you waited until everyone had caught up so that a collective decision could be taken about the correct route, and thus everyone stayed together. Gareth went back, all of 30 km, where he copped an earful from the others about breaching the etiquette. This didn't endear Rick to him any further, nor did it help to resolve tensions in the group. At least we got a run on the superhighway that day, as we were causing so much of a hold-up on the secondary roads that one of the tollgate officials waved us up onto the tarmac. Poor old Selwyn got clobbered by the barrier arm as he passed through.

But no matter how bad a day had been, and no matter how tired or pissed off anyone was at day's end, we always shared a beer in the evening. And somehow, sitting down and laughing at it all ironed out the wrinkles. The testy bits were quick to pass.

That night, we were in Langzhou, where we had an early night in readiness for an early start the next morning. At 7.30 am, we were welcomed by the students at the Langzhou language school. The reception was huge, with the whole school assembled for the daily flag-raising ceremony and great banners hung about town hailing the Silk Riders. There was a media contingent, even a television presence, there to watch us. We observed the lessons — these kids work like dogs, from seven in the morning to ten at night, with two hours off for lunch. It's little wonder they regularly fall asleep during class.

It's a cool place, with a strong New Zealand connection. Three of the teachers, Paul Burgin, Jane Ayres and Richard Keeling, hail from Christchurch. That evening, they took us out for a night on the tiles. It was quite an eye-opener, like being in Hong Kong in the 1990s, or Auckland in the 1980s. The kids all go about in fashionable Western clothes and hang out in glittering malls, featuring outlets for every imaginable major label. We wondered what Rewi Alley would have made of the new China, with all its conspicuous consumerism.

After the dreamlike ride along the highway the day before, we were back among the hay-wagons and pushbarrows the next day. We had further trouble with Rick, too. This time, it was his turn to get lost. We got separated from him when we reached a tract of grid-locked traffic, which we were better able to negotiate on our bikes than Rick and Jim in the Land Cruiser. We managed to navigate without him by consulting Dave's fancy GPS, and safely arrived at our lunch destination without him. We had a 'point and hope' lunch (when you can't speak the language, the only way to cope in restaurants where the menu ranges into the realms of what you might call the 'exotic' is to point at someone else's food and hope it's as edible as it looks), observed by a few journalists and 70-odd other people, few of whom had seen Westerners before, let alone in their village. Babies screamed at the sight of us; grannies pointed and cackled. After a bit of a rest, we raised Rick on his cellphone. By this time, he had nearly caught us up. As soon as he'd got separated, he just asked people along the way if they'd seen us. Six strangely dressed big-noses on bikes: we weren't very hard to track. He arrived, flustered and relieved all at once. Poor old Rick. Over the month we were with him, he broke out in acne on several occasions, which we put down to a reaction either to something he was eating or to the large quantities of alcohol he seemed to need to consume after a day of trying to explain Chinese rules and regulations to a bunch of Kiwi bikers. Looking back, it was probably stress.

We had all been on the toilet half the night, with a bit of a flare-up of the Silk Road squirts sweeping the group. They believe in karma in Buddhist parts of the world, and around this time, we saw it in action. As the rest of us had sickened with the squirts though Central Asia, Dave had bragged repeatedly that he had been passed over. He went noticeably quiet on the subject somewhere southwest of Langzhou, and it became obvious to anyone with an olfactory function that he, too, was now officially a victim of the Silk Road squirts. He sat rigid on his bike at one of our stops, refusing to dismount.

'How far is the hotel?' he asked.

'About five hours,' we replied.

'I'm not moving from this bike until we get there,' he vowed.

He was, by unanimous vote, consigned to the rear of the riding order until we found a laundry. Poor bugger. Even when we reached Pingliang, the day's destination, we found the hotel showers were heated only in the evenings. He had to clean up under cold water.

We had a good meal for about $1.20 per person that night, and we sent and received emails from a colossal internet café packed with about 400 people.

Some Chinese petrol stations had strange rules. Commonly you're not actually allowed to run your motor within 50 m of the pumps, let alone in the forecourt: you have to coast in, or push your vehicle. And the first couple of times we went to put the filler nozzle directly in the bikes' tanks, attendants would emerge from their sheds, yelling at us. It turned out they required us to fill a bucket from the pump then fill our bike from the bucket, so as to reduce the chances of the ignition of the petrol vapour during transfer by a spark from the static electricity induced by moving through all that hot, dry, ionising air. Seemed like far-fetched crap to us, but a few — thankfully only a few — attendants were precious about it.

The following day, we rolled into Xian (pronounced 'she-an'), which was the capital of China until Kublai Khan — Marco's 'Great Khan' — shifted it to Beijing in the 14th century. Today it's a thoroughly modern city with a population roughly half as large again as New

Zealand's. We went for a day trip from here to the famous 'terracotta warriors', the army of 2000-year-old, life-sized, life-like warriors guarding a royal tomb that was discovered in 1974 by a farmer digging a well. Since their discovery, a number of the warriors have been excavated, or at least the collapsed building that once housed them has been excavated, allowing a few divisions of the pottery figures to be painstakingly pieced together. It was gob-smacking to see them, the level of detail on every individual figure in that profusion of figures. It was even more amazing when you realise that only a fraction of the site has so far been excavated. They reckon 300,000 workers were used in the construction of this, the eighth wonder of the world, over the 35 years the project took, well over 2000 years ago.

The mechanical brains-trust decided the time had finally come to replace Bryan's chain, so Brendan got in contact with the BMW dealers in Hong Kong. They undertook to send a new chain up to us, the estimated time of its arrival about a week away.

Back in a *wang ba* — an internet café — in Xian city, Gareth got into a huff with Jo when she bought him only a ten-yuan card to cover his on-line needs. She didn't bother replying to him, leaving it up to him to work out, through a mixture of sign language and various pidgin tongues directed at a gang of assistants, that his ten yuan would last him ten hours on-line. It's so easy to lose sight of how cheap things are in this part of the world. Beer, for example, was the equivalent of NZ$1.20 a bottle. No wonder we all got on so well.

If he was in a huff over this, however, he was in a positive flap a little later, when he discovered that while he was absorbed in his dealings with the internet, a light-fingered local had made off with his i-mate. This was a huge loss, as by now it was crammed with pictures, details and information about the route we had taken and the things we had seen. Gareth was not a happy camper.

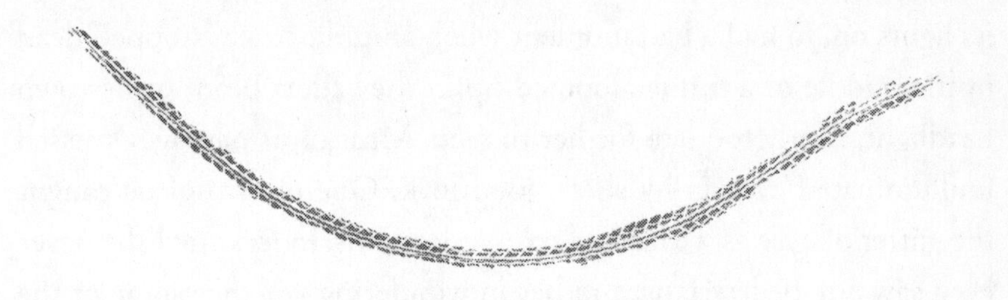

End of the road

From Xian, we pointed the bikes north and headed for Mongolia. It teemed down much of the day, which made things unpleasant in one respect. In another, it was a blessing, since we were again waved off the highway by tollgate officials, and the rain helped keep down the dust of the crappy minor roads we were forced to share with the other agricultural machinery. We wouldn't have had a show of getting out of town without local assistance, but we were eventually shown a sandy track that led to a decent road circumventing the tollgates. All the same, it was slow going. In our worst stretch, it took us two hours to travel a mere 25 km.

The minor roads wound their tortuous way around and alongside the superhighway, but every now and then, they ducked beneath it. The tunnels weren't lit. If you were riding in the middle of the group, you'd generally come across the front riders stopped and stashing their sunglasses in their pockets, peering gingerly into the tunnel's inky maw. All kinds of traffic sped out. A favoured method of navigating was to tuck in behind a vehicle with its tail-lights on, but this could be bloody disconcerting when you saw the red lights wobble out of the way of something oncoming on the wrong side of the carriageway.

And not everything speeding, weaving or limping its way through had its lights on. Jo had a bad moment when an unlit truck, stopped dead in the middle of a tunnel, loomed up in the yellow beam of her own headlight, nearly too late for her to stop. Most of us narrowly missed unilluminated cyclists by sheer good luck. One or two of us caught the glitter of eyes as we flashed past pedestrians. Jo reckoned she never even saw any pedestrians, and began wondering whether some of the larger bumps and jolts she'd felt had been potholes after all.

And it wasn't just the tunnels that made for demanding riding. Even out on the road, you had to have all your wits about you. There seemed to be a truck on your side of the road around every blind corner, as local drivers aren't too particular about where they execute their overtaking manoeuvres. And cars cruising past you would unceremoniously chop back into your lane, whether you were occupying it or not, at the sight of oncoming traffic. Much as we all liked Jim, there were times when his emotions got to him, and he would take us on a hair-raising ride through some of the towns, him speeding and weaving and us trying to keep up with him.

We survived and arrived in Luochuan very wet. Through Rick, the manager of the hotel where we intended to stay expressed concern about the security of our bikes. All the way across Central Asia, we'd made up our security routines as we went along. Mostly, we'd park near staff entrances, where hotel staff were coming and going all night. Two of the bikes were alarmed, so sometimes we'd chain them together with the alarmed bikes on the outside. Some of the hotels where we stayed were inside their own security perimeter, and even occasionally employed guards to patrol them. Here and there, we had the luxury of secure underground carparks.

The solution applied in Luochuan was novel. Dave jokingly suggested, through sign language, that perhaps the bikes would be safest in the hotel lobby. The woman agreed without a moment's hesitation. Quickly, and before she could change her mind, we scurried out and rode the bikes up the slippery marble steps, watched by a crowd of understandably curious locals. Our steeds looked great in their five-star accommodation, so we wasted no time in availing ourselves of the photo opportunity.

The next day, we passed through a little town where it was evidently market day, and caused chaos manoeuvring the bikes through the stalls and the crowd clogging the main through-road. We stopped just outside town, and Dave and Jo wandered back to get some fresh fruit. They discovered a crowd of two or three hundred people enjoying what they called 'a Chinese wailing concert' — the local music was an acquired taste — and they stopped to listen. Their arrival caused something of a stir, and soon the whole audience was looking at them. The singers lost the plot, and gave up as they peered over the heads of the crowd in an effort to see the aliens, too. Every face reflected total amazement. We were clearly off the beaten tourist track in these parts. People we talked to confirmed this. Many of them spoke excellent English, although this was the first chance, they told us, they'd had to use it outside the classroom.

Dave and Jo returned with bags of beautiful fresh apricots and apples. The produce in this part of the world was amazing, especially, for some reason, the tomatoes, which reminded all of us of the great, flavoursome 'beefsteak' varieties we remembered from our childhood.

We were speculating on the gardening secrets of people who grew the tomatoes we were enjoying one night, when Gareth suddenly looked stricken.

'No,' he said. 'It couldn't be, could it?'

'Couldn't be what?' asked Bryan.

'Well,' Gareth replied, 'without spelling it out, do you remember the joke about the two Remuera ladies talking about gardening? One asks the other, what do you put on your strawberries? Her friend replies that she puts horse manure on hers. The first one looks a bit horrified and says she puts cream on hers.'

We all looked at him blankly.

'Well,' Gareth shrugged, 'there are 1.3 billion Chinese. Work it out.'

We all looked at the tomatoes on our plates.

'I put salt on mine,' said Bryan.

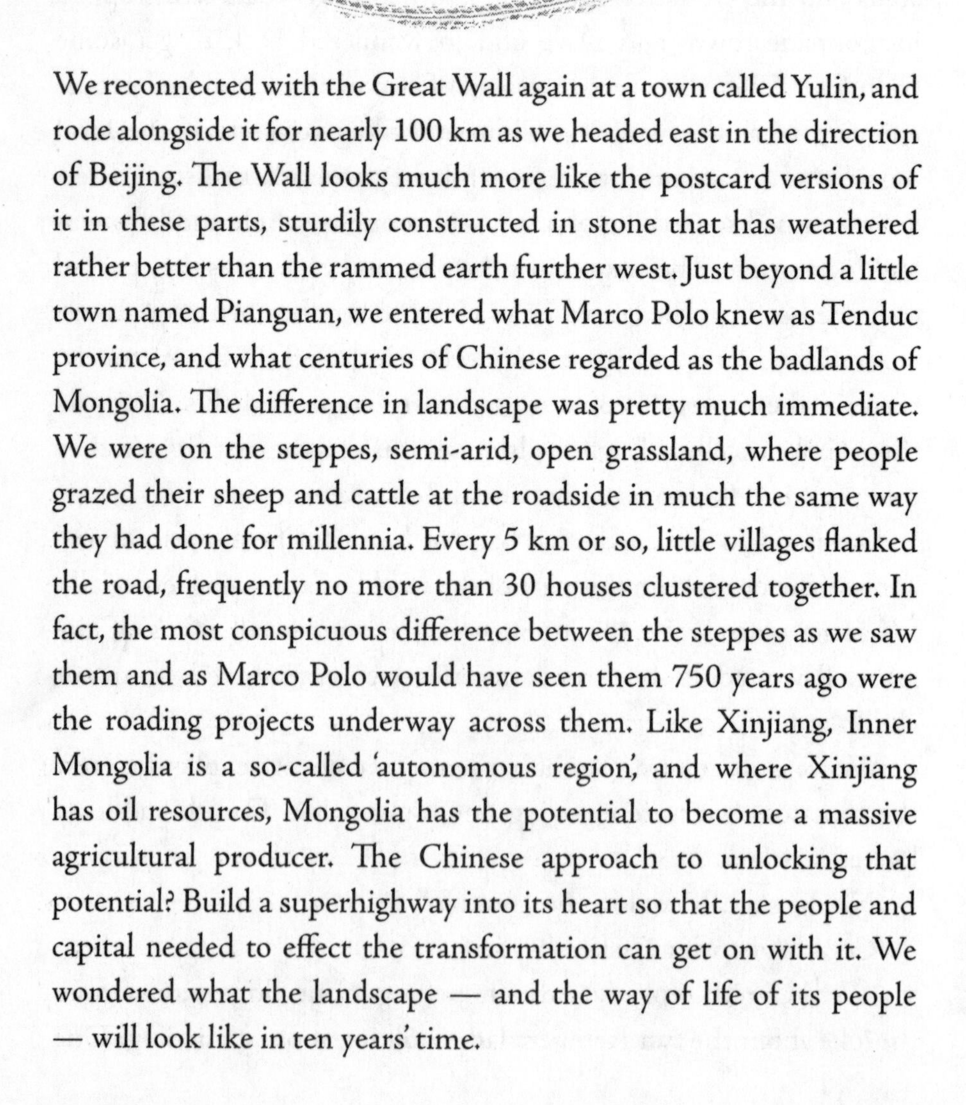

We reconnected with the Great Wall again at a town called Yulin, and rode alongside it for nearly 100 km as we headed east in the direction of Beijing. The Wall looks much more like the postcard versions of it in these parts, sturdily constructed in stone that has weathered rather better than the rammed earth further west. Just beyond a little town named Pianguan, we entered what Marco Polo knew as Tenduc province, and what centuries of Chinese regarded as the badlands of Mongolia. The difference in landscape was pretty much immediate. We were on the steppes, semi-arid, open grassland, where people grazed their sheep and cattle at the roadside in much the same way they had done for millennia. Every 5 km or so, little villages flanked the road, frequently no more than 30 houses clustered together. In fact, the most conspicuous difference between the steppes as we saw them and as Marco Polo would have seen them 750 years ago were the roading projects underway across them. Like Xinjiang, Inner Mongolia is a so-called 'autonomous region,' and where Xinjiang has oil resources, Mongolia has the potential to become a massive agricultural producer. The Chinese approach to unlocking that potential? Build a superhighway into its heart so that the people and capital needed to effect the transformation can get on with it. We wondered what the landscape — and the way of life of its people — will look like in ten years' time.

Roading projects in China are a sight to behold. They use modern machinery, but the resource they have in superabundance is the sheer number of people they can put on the end of a shovel. Thousands of them work alongside the bulldozers and earthmovers. In a matter of months, a road the quality of which New Zealanders can only dream about is conjured as if from nothing. Ask the locals what all the roads and motorways being built are in aid of, and they'll tell you it's all part of the preparations for the 2008 Olympic Games. There could be something in that, too.

At a little village in which we stopped, we got to see the peculiarly blurry line between the public and private lives of the Chinese. We had stopped at a restaurant and were sitting outside at a table, listening to a woman haranguing her husband inside. Every now and then she would emerge, and smilingly engage in a flurry of sign language with us to determine what we wanted to eat. Then she'd go back into the shop and resume her scolding and physical thrashing of hapless hubby where she'd left off. This establishment was memorable, too, for the small, fluffy dog under our table that sank its teeth into Selwyn's hand. What was his hand doing there you ask? Patting the cute fluffy mutt of course — impulsive insanity. No great damage was done, but we had a job persuading him to seek a booster on his rabies shots. We were able to pick up some grisly stories from the internet of what it's like to die of rabies, and these helped him to focus. He had the booster, and we were spared the prospect of dodging a rabid, frothing Selwyn a few days down the line.

At another of our lunch stops, Jo made the mistake of going into the kitchen. There was a middle-aged Chinese man, stripped to the waist, slaving over the wok in which our lunch was sizzling. Sweat was dripping from his round belly into the food. She shuddered, and withdrew from the grimy room, resolving to make do with fruit.

Our destination in Mongolia was Shangdu, which Marco knew as Xanadu and at which, according to Samuel Taylor Coleridge, Kublai Khan 'a stately pleasure-dome decreed'. Not that Coleridge knew much about it; he never went there, unless it was on the astral plane where a hit on his opium pipe had sent him. We had decreed something like a pleasure-dome there, too: it was marked on our spreadsheet itinerary as 'destination piss-up'.

Shangdu was easy enough to find on the maps. There it was, about 200 km northeast of Hohhot, the capital of Inner Mongolia. Simple.

Or so we thought. As we were cruising along toward it, we were surprised by the number of military vehicles — troop transports and assorted self-propelled artillery pieces — that we could see around us. The Chinese, we thought, are usually pretty touchy about showing off these particular toys. Strange, then, that we should be allowed along this road.

Sure enough, when we got to Shangdu itself — a decidedly unprepossessing town made according to the template of modern Chinese towns, with wall-to-wall white tiles and little joy or character to speak of — the powers seemed less than pleased to see us. In fact, we were directed to our hotel and then told we were forbidden to leave it until our improbable story could be checked out. Gareth had to make his scheduled media call to New Zealand from the fourth floor of the hotel, and sheepishly admit that we were in trouble with the authorities yet again.

It was hard work getting anyone in Shangdu to understand what we were trying to achieve. Today's Han Chinese are not big on Mongolian history, so Kublai Khan wasn't exactly a household name. Eventually, though, our mistake was discovered. Silly us — we had come to Shangdu. The place we wanted was Yuanshangdu, about 200 km away. Don't these big-noses know anything?

The next day, then, once we'd been allowed to leave, we turned our backs on 'False Shangdu', or 'Fool's Shangdu' as we came to call it, and cruised to Yuanshangdu, a ride we accomplished on a road that just about made up for all the rough surfaces we had endured on the trip. Soon after leaving, we were able to get onto a magnificent four-lane motorway, which was in the final stages of being completed. The tollgates had been installed but weren't manned, and there was hardly any traffic: in 200 km of smooth, easy riding, we counted eight cars, although there were a number of the ubiquitous three-wheeler trucks round and about. The motorway is elevated above the surrounding countryside, so we had a grandstand view of the steppes. Here and there, workers were putting the finishing touches to the stonework on cuttings. Each stone is individually cut to size and then placed by hand, and once the wall is in place, plasterers come in and point the gaps. The result is something like a giant, stone jigsaw — really quite beautiful.

There was nothing much to Yuanshangdu. Whereas Marco Polo described not one but two pleasure-domes there in the 13th century — a huge marble structure and a kind of wicker and linen porta-bach for those hot Mongolian summers — there's hardly a discernible trace today. Nevertheless, the locals pointed us to a set of likely looking ruins, chiefly the low, rounded and grass-covered remains of a wall that are preserved as the site of Kublai's imperial palace, and it was here that we sat down and pulled the cork on the bottle of Marco Polo wine we'd brought all the way from Korcula. While there were a few days left, this was the symbolic end of the journey: the eastern limit of Kublai Khan's empire, which stretched right back the way we had come, to Hungary. This was where, in 1275, Kublai Khan had received Niccolo and Maffeo Polo, and Niccolo's boy, Marco, to whom he took something of a shine. It also signified the end of the whole, massive Silk Riders enterprise. Since April, we had covered almost 20,000 km, crossed two major deserts, dodged through a couple of war zones and visited the three inland oceans of the Black Sea, the Caspian Sea and the Aral Sea. The bikes were all still going, and so were the bikers. We had braved hazards both natural and human, yet we were all still here, life and limb intact. We'd hardly had to use our first-aid skills — not a single limb was amputated, not a single gunshot wound plugged with a tampon. There were some niggling illnesses and injuries, the most serious of which was Jo's manhole episode. We'd spent a remarkable proportion of the time upright: you needed only the fingers of one hand to count the spills. More remarkably, we were all still talking to one another. We sat in the ruins and basked in the sense of a mission successfully accomplished.

'You realise,' Gareth said to everyone as we sat there, 'that we head south tomorrow. It's all over.'

We stared moodily into our glasses.

'But,' he went on, 'we could turn round, go north, head into Siberia and go round to Vladivostok. What d'you reckon? Should we do it?'

It had been a long, long trip. Everyone was missing friends and family. We'd had our ups, but we'd certainly had our downs. We'd all suffered some measure of physical deterioration — Dave, for example, had lost 15 kg. We were all worn down by the strain of concentrating so hard for such long hours, and by the effort of just trying to get by in countries where everything is different and people don't speak your language.

Even considering all that, everyone wanted to do it. No one was quite ready for the trip to be over. Brendan reckoned he'd have to get permission, and actually pulled out his i-mate and emailed his wife. She told him that so long as he could give her a date when he would, at last, be coming home, no problem.

'I'm up for it,' he said.

We kicked the idea around for a while, deadly serious, but upon due consideration, decided there was too much booked and locked down to disrupt. But it was irrefutable testimony to how good the trip had been, and how well we'd all got on.

The last leg of our trip involved a cruise down to Zhangjiakou, centre of the Great Wall of China souvenir industry. This section, a couple of hours from Beijing as the coach crawls, has been fully restored and snakes its picturesque way up and over bush-clad ridges. Rick had arranged accommodation for us, but when we saw it, we flatly refused to stay there. It was seedy as hell, and not much like somewhere we'd trust with the bikes or ourselves. Jo and Dave went off and located another, far better place and booked us in, obtaining a decent discount for the group at the same time. It seemed to confirm our dark suspicions of Rick's commission-agent approach to his job.

By now, Jo and Dave had figured out a way of avoiding the premium put on local prices by restaurants in the tourist areas. You'd grab a menu, persuade another diner to show you which item they were eating, then demand the local price. And curiously enough, by this end of the trip, the people in the group who seemed to have acquired the strongest aversion to paying more than was strictly necessary were the same ones who had scoffed at the notion of paying our own way at the outset.

We had traversed the Great Wall in its entirety from west to east, and we were up there at dawn, before the coaches arrived and disgorged the 21st-century equivalent of the Mongol hordes, the tourists. After taking the obligatory photographs and lamenting the lack of a view that we surmised must lie behind the smog, we saddled up and set off for Beijing, which was known as Khan-Balik, 'the Lord's City', in Kublai Khan's day. Marco described it as 'full of fine mansions, inns and dwelling-houses'. Those inns were sounding pretty good to us.

It was a relatively easy ride, although we were wary both of the traffic and of the well-known phenomenon of end-of-bike-tour lapses in rider concentration. It would, after all, seem a shame to have traversed the better part of 20,000 km only to die under a Chinese three-wheeler in the last 20.

Finishing the trip in the Chinese capital seemed an appropriate way to end it all, as there could be little doubt from what we had seen that this is the world capital-in-waiting. We hadn't even visited the vast country's economic and industrial powerhouse in the southeast, yet the signs of the speed and scale of the boom it is undergoing were everywhere. When you compare what's afoot in China with what is happening in the former states of the USSR, the 'stans to China's west . . . well, there's no comparison. As China storms toward world leadership, the benighted and abused countries to the west will be left in its dust. Even India, from what we had seen on previous trips, although it too has vast human resources, cannot hope to hold a candle to the Chinese colossus. You have to wonder whether in India this is partly because half those resources lie idle: it seems to be the women who do the work there, as in Central Asia, while the men squat around smoking and talking.

We cruised down the highway toward Beijing, the traffic getting denser by the mile. At some point as we were in the outskirts of the glittering, bustling capital of China, Rick and Jim guided us into a complex not unlike a New Zealand vehicle-testing station. After a discussion with the officials, Rick told us we needed to turn around and go back to get the necessary permissions to proceed. We'd already over-reached our official welcome: Beijing is surrounded by several ring-roads, and we needed permission to proceed to each. We had permissions for the fifth ring, but here we were at the fourth.

Bugger that, we told him. If you care that much, you go back.

Rick assumed the politely pained expression with which we'd become so familiar over the last month. He and Jim had a stand-up row, which ended with Jim heading back out to the fifth ring-road to get permission. Rick got up behind Brendan, and we rode to our hotel in the third ring. Jim eventually showed up with permission for us to ride in the fourth ring. No way was he going back again: we would have to take our chances.

Here we were, then, in Beijing, with its skyline forested with cranes and the dust of a million construction projects hanging in the air, in the early afternoon of Friday, July 8. We dressed for dinner — or at least, Jo and Bryan did, as they'd carried their evening wear with them all 20,000 km. Bryan had a white shirt and black tie; Jo had a silk dress which she matched with a pair of hastily purchased shoes, and was rewarded with blank stares when she first appeared, clean and dressed like a woman for the first time in months.

That evening, Tony Browne, the New Zealand ambassador to China, hosted a reception for us at the embassy. The local BMW agent was there to welcome us, and presented us each with a BMW T-shirt. Members of the local BMW owners' club had turned out in force, and there was a large contingent of other invited guests from the local and expatriate communities. A band from St Peter's College in Auckland, which was in Beijing to perform a number of concerts, was there too, and they provided a bill of very passable big-band 'standards', which were well received by all present. There was also a big feed laid on by the chef and staff at the embassy, washed down with stunning Kiwi wine and all served at tables beautifully set out on the lawn.

We enjoyed ourselves immensely, each of us conscious, now that we'd reached our ultimate destination and no longer had to worry even about the bikes, of how big a responsibility had been lifted from our shoulders. That's the price of playing in a team: everyone has a stake in the collective enterprise, and it's only when the team's goals are realised that every individual can allow themselves to feel satisfied. What a great team effort it had been.

At about 11 pm, we made our way out to the road to hail a couple of taxis to take us back to our hotel. Suddenly, the tranquillity of the quiet, tree-lined street was shattered by a loud roar, the unmistakeable sound of the unmuffled exhaust of a motorcycle.

Down the road, a bike and sidecar appeared, ridden with great style and skill by a barefoot, bareheaded young lady with her blond hair and white summer coat blowing in the slipstream and a young female passenger hanging on in the sidecar. She roared up and braked hard, tyres smoking, outside the embassy. Dave and Brendan needed no encouragement to add themselves to the outfit, one on the pillion seat and the other squeezed into the sidecar. Then it was clutch out and they were off, that coat flying in their wake.

What the hell was that? we wondered, even as we resigned ourselves to seeing nothing of Brendan and Dave before morning — even supposing the catastrophic noise of the exhaust failed to draw the attention of the local police to the bike with its four-up. Five minutes later, though, just as we were getting ourselves organised into taxis, the bike and all four occupants appeared at the end of the embassy road with a noise like thunder. It blasted down the road and screeched to a halt as before, pausing only long enough to let the slightly dazed-looking Dave and Brendan off, before disappearing up the road. It turned a corner, and the silence after the roar of the open exhaust was shocking.

'Who's she?' Gareth asked the ambassador

'Never seen her before in my life,' he shrugged.

'Oh. It's just that she and the young lady in the sidecar were at the reception,' Gareth said.

'Maybe so,' Browne replied, 'but they weren't invited.'

Talking to some of the Chinese BMW owners, we learned that

Rebecca and her immaculate black Chang Jiang (a copy of the Russian Ural, which in turn is a copy of a pre-war BMW made from designs passed to Russia as part of the Second World War reparations. It has a side-valve, 750 cc, horizontally opposed, twin-cylinder engine and shaft drive and is still made in China) are a legend in Beijing. She always rides fast, always at night and is always dressed in her white summer coat. She had gatecrashed our diplomatic reception at the suggestion of the local BMW boys. We never did find out the name of her sidecar passenger, who had gatecrashed too. What we did learn, though, was that according to consensus, Rebecca is not a girl at all; but she was a decent facsimile, especially in the eyes of boys after a boozy night and a long, long, solitary trip.

The next day, the last of the trip, we had a look around Beijing, visiting the old city with the narrow streets that were laid out by Kublai Khan himself. In the evening, we visited the Lugou Bridge — otherwise known as the Marco Polo bridge — with its long lines of stone lions. We rounded the night off with a moderately riotous celebration at that most Chinese of institutions, an Irish pub. The next day, we broke the very last of the countless rules and regulations that we had trampled underfoot en route: we rode from the hotel to the packing company's premises in the third ring without a permit.

We said our farewells to Rick and Jim, and gave them a tip after all. Was it our imagination, or were their smiles slightly strained, and the regret they expressed at seeing us go just a trifle lacking in sincerity? Whatever, we bet Rick's skin has cleared up nicely by now, and that he will forever have second thoughts when he's asked to guide Kiwi bikers.

Then, the plane. There's nothing like settling back into an airline seat and, after the thrill of the acceleration, seeing the ground falling away beneath you to set a full-stop on a trip like this, where we had been so intimately in contact with the ground every step of the 20,000 km from where it all began.

Marco Polo said on his deathbed in 1324, 'I have not told you the half of what I saw'. We felt mighty privileged to have traced his footsteps, though we felt we had but scratched the surface of what we could have seen if we'd taken four years, as he did, to get there.

Acknowledgements

This journey took a lot of planning and there are many people we need to thank for their efforts in making it happen. Top of the list come our fellow riders Dave, Bryan, Brendan, Phil and Selwyn, who all shouldered their share — and more at times — to keep the show on the road. Above all, they were fun to be with. And the one we left at home, Mike O'Donnell, did heaps to make this thing happen and his efforts were appreciated greatly by all.

The construction and maintenance of the *www.silkriders.com* website was important to the trip. Many thanks to Dave Bruce and Michael Bordignon from Gareth's office in Wellington, for dealing to the seemingly endless stream of requests from both the Riders and the public for site enhancements and further information.

Then there are our business partners. Firstly, thank you to BMW, whose participation revealed a business culture that was exemplary, assisting us far beyond what was expected and in remote parts of the world where we didn't expect them to be. Particular thanks to BMW agent Sanar Motors in Tashkent and its owner Mirmahdi, who provided a facility and technical assistance without which we would have had to ship one bike home early.

Next, thanks to the folks at Fairydown, Vodafone and Lufthansa, who all helped with specialist supplies. We'd like to commend their patience with our ever-changing needs. Icebreaker, John Baker Insurance, Metzeler, Scottoiler, Tony Rees Motorcycles, Silk Road Adventures and Marvelox all played strong support roles. Pat and Murray Reedy of Silk Road Adventures made a commendable effort to accommodate the idiosyncratic needs of a motorcycling group trying to traverse countries simply not used to that type of visitor.

Tony Browne, New Zealand's ambassador in Beijing, was a marvellous host for our arrival at journey's end and numerous staff of Foreign Affairs were most helpful in assisting us to negotiate our way out of trouble with foreign bureaucrats.

Thanks to our family for putting up with what they see as the irrational whims of a couple of ageing hippies, who seemed in an indecent hurry to 'leave home' within an hour of our youngest child Ruby's departure for boarding school. We can only say it was purely coincidental; we had to go when we had to go, abandoned children or not.

And last, but in no way least, to John McCrystal, the writer who crafted this manuscript based on some pretty rushed and interrupted interviews with us. Sorry, John, for being so unstable. What with planning the next trips, and squeezing a year's work and family time into six months, there's never enough time to give the last expedition justice.

Bring on the next ride.

Gareth and Jo Morgan

unicef

The authors' proceeds from this book are going to the UNICEF project in Kyrgyzstan sponsored by the Silk Riders.

Author profiles

Gareth Morgan

Economist, portfolio investor, motorcycle adventurer and chronically addicted fisherman — Gareth has never really fitted well with the mainstream but his larger-than-life persona has won him many fans and more than a few foes. If nothing else, applying the blowtorch of economic theory to expose sector interests acting against national wellbeing tends to cause a reaction.

For all that, he has instigated two successful and well-known New Zealand businesses: the economics consultancy Infometrics, and Gareth Morgan Investments (www.garethmorgan.com), his personal portfolio management business.

Joanne (Jo) Morgan

Arguably the saner of the pair, Jo's adult life has spanned a spectrum of interests — from welding to social work, importing (when New Zealand was trade-protected and profit margins were to die for), bus driving, teaching, studying languages, and mechanical repairs. Oh, and besides all that she brought up four children and ran a home as Gareth travelled New Zealand spreading the economic word.

Jo tied to expose her young children early to the realities of others' lives: in Smokey Mountain, Manila; on the Afghanistan–Pakistan border in the Hindu Kush; and in Korean primary schools. She hoped this would also foster in them a love of travel and appreciation of other cultures.

These days, in a space few females are prepared to enter, Jo's motorcycling exploits have seen her handstanding on her bike while crossing the salt pans of Bolivia, trading in the floating flower-market on Dal Lake in Kashmir, rock-hopping an Enfield up the Himalayan slopes of Nepal, and plummeting down the world's most dangerous road in Bolivia.

Her enthusiasm for the extraordinary has not dampened her commitment to her home, and Jo continues to play an active role in the politics and life of her local community.

Now with a grown-up family, Gareth and Jo — when not doting on their new granddaughter — have widened their activities to roaming the globe, which enables Gareth to experience first-hand the businesses, societies and economies his portfolios are invested in.

The details of their global traverse by motorcycle are recorded on *www.worldbybike.com*